# Moodle 1.9 Top Extensions Cookbook

Over 60 simple and incredibly effective recipes for harnessing the power of the best Moodle modules to create effective online learning sites

**Michael de Raadt**

PUBLISHING

BIRMINGHAM - MUMBAI

# Moodle 1.9 Top Extensions Cookbook

First published: November 2010

Production Reference: 1021110

Published by Packt Publishing Ltd.
32 Lincoln Road
Olton
Birmingham, B27 6PA, UK.

ISBN 978-1-849512-16-9

www.packtpub.com

Cover Image by Ed Maclean (edmaclean@gmail.com)

# Credits

**Author**

Michael de Raadt

**Reviewers**

Mary Cooch

Ben Reynolds

**Acquisition Editor**

Usha Iyer

**Development Editor**

Meeta Rajani

**Technical Editor**

Sakina Kaydawala

**Indexer**

Tejal Daruwale

**Editorial Team Leader**

Mithun Sehgal

**Project Team Leader**

Ashwin Shetty

**Project Coordinator**

Zainab Bagasrawala

**Proofreader**

Jacqueline McGhee

**Production Coordinator**

Adline Swetha Jesuthas

**Cover Work**

Adline Swetha Jesuthas

# About the Author

**Michael de Raadt** is a regular family guy who lives in Toowoomba, in the state of Queensland, Australia. He enjoys camping, hiking, and playing table tennis. Michael is also a Cub Scout leader.

In his professional life, Michael wears a number of hats. He is a lecturer in Computing Science (usually teaching programming), he is a researcher of educational technology, and a developer of Moodle modules. He currently works at the University of Southern Queensland where he is an advisor on teaching and learning matters. Michael holds a PhD which he gained through research in computing education and has published numerous papers in this research area.

Michael enjoys being a member of the Moodle Community. He helps out with the management of modules contributed to Moodle. Within his local area, Michael is an advocate for development of modules for Moodle.

I would like to thank my family for supporting me during the writing of this book. I would also like to acknowledge the community of developers who have contributed the modules reviewed in this book, and acknowledge Anthony Borrow, who has generously offered his time overseeing such contributions.

# About the Reviewers

**Mary Cooch** (known online as the Moodlefairy) is a teacher, VLE trainer specializing in Moodle and the author of Packt's *Moodle 1.9 For Teaching 7-14 Year Olds* and *Moodle 2.0 First Look*. She is based at Our Lady's Catholic High School, Preston, Lancashire, UK and can be contacted for training and consultancy on `mco@olchs.lancs.sch.uk`.

Thanks, both to my family at home and to Mark at school for their support.

**Ben Reynolds** is a Senior Program Manager of CTYOnline at the Johns Hopkins University's Center for Talented Youth (CTY). An award-winning fictionist, he began CTY's face-to-face writing program in 1978 and launched CTYOnline's writing program in 1983. He began administrating CTYOnline's writing and language arts division in 1985. CTYOnline serves over 10,000 students a year in writing/language arts, math, science, computer science, advanced placement, and foreign languages. In the 1990's, Reynolds left the classroom for full-time administration of both CTY's writing/language arts program and of a residential site for CTY Summer Programs. Reynolds has also taught writing and the teaching of writing for the Johns Hopkins School of Continuing Studies. He holds a BA from Duke University, where he part-timed in the computer center, trading printouts for punch cards, and an MA from Johns Hopkins in Fiction Writing. He is an active member of the Using Moodle community.

# Table of Contents

# **Preface**

Moodle is growing at a seemingly unstoppable rate. One of the key reasons for Moodle's popularity is its potential to be extended with modules. This book will teach you how to find the best Moodle modules, how to install them, how to configure them, and how to get the most out of them.

There are hundreds of Moodle modules available. Find out which you can trust and how to put them to work.

This book is written to help you find modules that will be useful to you and your students, and to show examples of how these modules can be set up and used in teaching.

## **What this book covers**

*Chapter 1, Getting Modular with Moodle,* is an introduction to adding contributed modules to a Moodle instance including how to find, install, and remove modules; related matters of site-wide settings, languages, and bugs are also discussed.

*Chapter 2, Adding Content,* discusses modules useful for adding various forms of content that a teacher may use with students.

*Chapter 3, Connecting to the Outside World,* talks about modules that allow students to access real-world resources outside of Moodle.

*Chapter 4, Getting Around In Moodle,* introduces handy modules that assist in navigating within and between courses in a Moodle site, also making Moodle more accessible to the visually impaired.

*Chapter 5, Effective Use of Space,* discusses modules that allow screen real-estate to be better used, including collapsing content.

*Chapter 6, Assessing Students,* discusses simple and novel modules that assist in assessing students.

*Chapter 7, Organizing Students*, talks about modules that assist in organizing students into groups and peer relationships, helping students with time-management, and getting feedback from students.

*Chapter 8, Encouraging Student Interaction*, introduces handy modules that allow students to interact in a common workspace and communicate more effectively.

*Chapter 9, Informing Students* talks about modules used to communicate information that is not related to regular material or assessment.

*Chapter 10, Handy Tools for Teachers*, discusses modules that aid and inform teachers in their tasks, such as creating activities and finding information and statistics about students.

*Chapter 11, Just for Fun*, ends the book with non-essential modules that make learning more enjoyable for students.

# What you need for this book

If you wish to test the modules presented in this book you will need the following:

- A web server
- A Moodle instance

Windows and Mac users can download packages from `http://download.moodle.org/` that contain both of these ingredients combined. Alternately, you can download Moodle separately from the preceding link and add it to a web server such as XAMPP (`http://www.apachefriends.org/en/xampp.html`).

More information about setting up and managing your test server can be found in *Chapter 1, Getting Modular with Moodle*.

# Who this book is for

This book is primarily aimed at readers who are involved with teaching using Moodle. This includes the following:

- Teachers at relatively small institutions running their own Moodle instance
- Teachers at large institutions where Moodle is used and administered
- Administrators of a Moodle instance who are looking for modules that will be useful to teachers and students at their institution

Some of the topics covered in this book are specific and technical, but directions will always be provided. No programming ability is needed to add and install Moodle modules.

# Conventions

In this book, you will find a number of styles of text that distinguish between different kinds of information. Here are some examples of these styles, and an explanation of their meaning.

Code words in text are shown as follows: "Unzip and copy the `birthday` block directory."

A block of code is set as follows:

```
<object width="190">
<param name="movie" value="http://localhost/moodle/file.php/2/
invaders.swf">
<embed src="http://localhost/moodle/file.php/2/invaders.swf"
width="190">
</embed>
</object>
```

**New terms** and **important words** are shown in bold. Words that you see on the screen, in menus or dialog boxes for example, appear in the text like this: "You will then be able to add the **Session Theme** block from the **Blocks** menu."

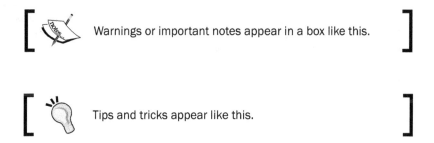

[ Warnings or important notes appear in a box like this. ]

[ Tips and tricks appear like this. ]

# Reader feedback

Feedback from our readers is always welcome. Let us know what you think about this book— what you liked or may have disliked. Reader feedback is important for us to develop titles that you really get the most out of.

To send us general feedback, simply send an e-mail to feedback@packtpub.com, and mention the book title via the subject of your message.

If there is a book that you need and would like to see us publish, please send us a note in the **SUGGEST A TITLE** form on www.packtpub.com or e-mail suggest@packtpub.com.

If there is a topic that you have expertise in and you are interested in either writing or contributing to a book, see our author guide on www.packtpub.com/authors.

# Customer support

Now that you are the proud owner of a Packt book, we have a number of things to help you to get the most from your purchase.

## Errata

Although we have taken every care to ensure the accuracy of our content, mistakes do happen. If you find a mistake in one of our books—maybe a mistake in the text or the code—we would be grateful if you would report this to us. By doing so, you can save other readers from frustration and help us improve subsequent versions of this book. If you find any errata, please report them by visiting `http://www.packtpub.com/support`, selecting your book, clicking on the **errata submission form** link, and entering the details of your errata. Once your errata are verified, your submission will be accepted and the errata will be uploaded on our website, or added to any list of existing errata, under the Errata section of that title. Any existing errata can be viewed by selecting your title from `http://www.packtpub.com/support`.

## Piracy

Piracy of copyright material on the Internet is an ongoing problem across all media. At Packt, we take the protection of our copyright and licenses very seriously. If you come across any illegal copies of our works, in any form, on the Internet, please provide us with the location address or website name immediately so that we can pursue a remedy.

Please contact us at `copyright@packtpub.com` with a link to the suspected pirated material.

We appreciate your help in protecting our authors, and our ability to bring you valuable content.

## Questions

You can contact us at `questions@packtpub.com` if you are having a problem with any aspect of the book, and we will do our best to address it.

# 1
# Getting Modular with Moodle

In this chapter, we will cover:

- ▸ Accessing Moodle plugins
- ▸ Adding and installing modules
- ▸ Changing site-wide settings
- ▸ Getting modules to speak your language
- ▸ Reporting bugs and suggesting improvements
- ▸ Removing modules

## Introduction

Moodle is an open source **Learning Management System** (**LMS**). If you're reading this book, it's likely that you are already using Moodle, or you have heard about it.

Image source: `http://moodle.org/`.

The word Moodle is actually an acronym. The 'M' in Moodle stands for Modular and the modularity of Moodle has been one of the key aspects of its success. Being modular means you can:

- ▸ Add modules to your Moodle instance
- ▸ Selectively use the modules you need

**M.O.O.D.L.E.**

The acronym Moodle stands for Modular Object-Oriented Dynamic Learning Environment. It is modular because you can add and remove modules. The programming paradigm used to create Moodle code is Object-Oriented. It is dynamic because it can be used for information delivery and interactivity, in a changeable and flexible way. It is a learning environment designed for teaching at many levels.

Because Moodle is modular and open source, many people have created modules for Moodle, and many of those modules are available freely for you to use. At time of writing, there are over 600 modules that you can download from the Moodle **Modules and plugins** database. Some of these are popular, well designed, and well maintained modules. Others are ideas that didn't seem to get off the ground. Some are contributed and maintained by large institutions, but most are contributed by individuals, often teachers themselves, who want to share what they have created.

If you have an idea for something you would like to do with Moodle, it's possible that someone has had that idea before and has created and shared a module you can use. This chapter will show you how to download and test contributed Moodle modules, to see if they suit your needs. Later chapters will help you find modules that will be useful to you and your students, and to show examples of how these modules can be set up and used in teaching.

**Origins of Moodle**

Moodle began in 1999 as postgraduate work of Martin Dougiamas, "out of frustration with the existing commercial software at the time". Considering the widespread use of Moodle around the world (over 40,000 registered sites in over 200 countries), Martin is a very humble man. If you ever make it to a MoodleMoot and Martin is in attendance, be sure to introduce yourself.

## A test server

If you only want to test modules, consider setting up your own basic web server, such as XAMPP (http://www.apachefriends.org/en/xampp.html) and installing Moodle from the Moodle **Downloads** page (http://download.moodle.org/). If you are a Windows or Mac user, you can even download and install Moodle packages where these two ingredients are already combined and ready to go.

Once installed, add a course or two. Create some dummy students to see how modules work within a course. Have a play around with the modules available—Moodle is quite hard to break—don't be afraid to experiment.

# Getting modules you can trust

The Moodle **Modules and plugins** database is filled with modules great and small. This book will review a range of useful modules and show you how to use them, but first you may want to know how you can find modules yourself.

It is helpful to know where the modules discussed in this book come from, and how they were judged as worthy candidates for review.

## Getting ready

You may have an idea in mind, or you may just want to see what's out there. You'll need a web browser and an active Internet connection.

## How to do it...

Point your browser to the Moodle **Modules and plugins** database. Refer `http://moodle.org/mod/data/view.php?id=6009`:

Image source: `http://moodle.org/mod/data/view.php?id=6009.`

As you scroll down you will see list of modules that can be downloaded. At the bottom of the page is a **Search** facility:

Image source: `http://moodle.org/mod/data/view.php?id=6009.`

You can also try an advanced search to get more specific about the following:

▶ What type of module you want

▶ What version of Moodle you have

▶ A number of other features

The following is a search result for the term 'progress':

Found records: 21/626 (Reset filters)

Page: 1 2 3 (Next)

| Name | Type | Requires | Summary | |
| --- | --- | --- | --- | --- |
| Checklist | Activity Module | Moodle 1.9 | Allows a student's progress to be tracked by the teacher and the student | 🔍 |
| Enhanced File Module (multiple uploads) | Resource Type | Moodle 1.9 or later | Enhanced File Resource Module – upload multiple files in one go | 🔍 |
| Progress Tracker | Small Hack | Moodle 1.9 | a hack of the Topic Course Format that displays a tickbox next to resources | 🔍 |
| Trackpad (Todo lists) | Activity Module | Moodle 1.9 or later | A task list / todo list activity | 🔍 |
| Offline Moodle: Google Gears caching | Integration | Moodle 2.0 or later | Offline caching integration using Google Gears | 🔍 |
| Progress Bar | Block | Moodle 1.9 | A time management tool for you and your students | ✎ ✗ 🔍 |
| MoodleCAP | Activity Module | Moodle 1.8 or later | Controls and management for class assistance. | 🔍 |
| Quiz Report Analysis | Major Patch | Moodle 1.8 or later | A new kind of quiz reports with rich text and detailed graphs. Analysis of student performance is both per attempt and per question category. | 🔍 |
| MoodleReader Module | Activity Module | Moodle 1.9 or later | Interface for controlling access to Extensive Reading Quizzes | 🔍 |
| QUESTOURnament module | Activity Module | Moodle 1.7 or later | Organize both individual and group contests in your course.. | 🔍 |

Page: 1 2 3 (Next)

Entries per page 10 ⌄   Search progress      Sort by Time added ⌄ Descending ⌄   ☐ Advanced search   Save settings

Image source: `http://moodle.org/mod/data/view.php?id=6009`.

Each entry has a type, the version of Moodle that it is compatible with, and a brief description. Clicking on the name of the module will take you to a page with details about the module. This is the module's 'entry':

Image source: `http://moodle.org/mod/data/view.php?d=13&rid=2524&filter=1`.

On each entry page there is a wealth of information about the module. The following is a list of questions you will want to answer when determining if the module is worth testing.

- Will it work with your version of Moodle?
- Is documentation provided?
- When was the module released and has there been activity (postings on the page below) since then?
- Is the module author active in the discussion about the module?

- Is the discussion positive (don't be too discouraged by bug reports if the author is involved and reporting that bugs have been fixed)?

- From discussion, can you tell if the module is widely used with a community of users behind it?

- What is the rating of the module?

If you are happy with your answers to these questions, then you may have found a useful module.

 Be wary of modules that do what you want, but are not supported; you may be wasting your time and putting the security of your system and the integrity your teaching at risk.

## There's more...

Here is some additional information that may help you on a module hunt.

### Types of modules

In order to get a sense of how modules will work, you need to have an understanding of the distinction between different module types. The following table describes common module types. Amid the array of modules available, the majority are blocks and activity modules.

| | |
|---|---|
| **Activity module** | Activity modules deliver information or facilitate interactivity within a course. Links to activity modules are added on a course main page and the activity module itself appears on a new page when clicked. Examples in the core installation are 'Forums' and 'Quizzes'. |
| **Assignment type** | Assignment types are a specific type of activity module that focus on assessable work. They are all based on a common assignment framework and appear under 'Assignments' in the activities list. Examples in the core installation are 'Advanced upload of files' and 'Online text' assignments. |
| **Block** | Blocks usually appear down each side of a course main page. They are usually passive, presenting specific information, and links to more information and activities. A block is a simpler type of module. Because they are easy to create, there are a large number of these in the **Modules and plugins** database. Examples in the core installation are the 'Calendar' and 'Online Users' blocks. |

| Course format | A course format allows the structure of a course main page to be changed to reflect the nature of the delivery of the course, for example, by schedule or by topic. |
|---|---|
| **Filter** | Filters allow targeted text appearing around a Moodle site to be replaced with other content, for example, equations, videos, or audio clips. |
| **Integration** | An integration module allows Moodle to make use of systems outside the Moodle instance itself. |
| **Question type** | Within a quiz, question types can be added to enable different forms of questions to be asked. |

## Checking your version

If you are setting up your own Moodle instance for teaching or just for testing, take note of the version you are installing.

If you have access to the **Site Administration** interface (the Moodle site root page when logged in as an administrator), clicking on Notifications will show you the version number near the bottom, for example **Moodle 1.9.8 (Build: 20100325)**. The first part of this is the Moodle version; this is what you need when searching through modules on the **Modules and plugins** database. The second part, labeled "Build" shows the date when the installed version was released in YYYYMMDD format. This version information reflects what is stored in the /version.php file.

If you are not the administrator of your system, consult the person who is. They should usually be able to tell you the version without looking it up.

**Moodle 2.0**

The next version of Moodle to follow version 1.9 has been "on the cards" for some time. At time of writing, only preview versions of Moodle 2.0 have been released. The process of installing modules will not change in the new version, so most of the information in this book will still be valid. You will need to look for versions of modules ready for Moodle 2.0 as earlier versions will not work without adjustment. As modules are usually contributed by volunteers, there may be some waiting before this happens; the best way to encourage this re-development is to suggest an improvement for the module on the Moodle bug tracker system at http://tracker.moodle.org/.

## See also

▸   Adding modules to Moodle

# Adding modules to Moodle

Once you've found a module you would like to test, you need to know how to add and install that module.

## Getting ready

You will need to have your web server running with Moodle installed. If you are not an administrator of the site, you will need assistance from someone who is.

To install a module, you will need to access your file browser to copy files and a web browser to see the results. You will need to be able to unzip files as this is how files in a module are packaged together.

## How to do it...

On the entry page for the module, look for the links at the bottom-right of the description. If you have an older version of Moodle, look for the version of the module that is suitable for your version.

```
                            Documentation
                              Browse CVS
                               Changelog
                              Discussion
                      Download latest version
                      Download for Moodle 1.9
                      Download for Moodle 1.8
                           Bugs and Issues

nard - Saturday, 11 April 2009, 07:05 AM
ed - Thursday, 27 August 2009, 01:31 AM
```

Image source: `http://moodle.org/mod/data/view.php?d=13&rid=2524&filter=1.`

Clicking on the link will take you to a new page, then a download dialog should appear. Most modules are packaged as `zip` files. Save the `zip` file to an easily accessible location on your computer.

As a specific example, search for the Progress Bar block in the Moodle **Modules and plugins** database. Find the download link and download the file. The filename should be `progress.zip`.

Once you have the file downloaded on your machine, you need to unzip the code and copy it to a location within the Moodle file structure. The location for the files will depend on the type of module you are installing.

 A `zip` file is a collection of files that have been combined together into a single file and compressed. How you "unzip" a file will depend on your operating system. Most operating systems will provide support to unzip. Try double clicking on a `zip` file and you may be presented with a view of its contents; dragging the files from such a view will uncompress and copy the files from the `zip` into the location you drop them. If this doesn't work for you, try right-clicking on the `zip` file and see what options are available for extracting the files inside.

The following table shows where common module types need to be placed within the Moodle file structure. You will need to know where the Moodle code exists within the file structure of your server when viewed using your file browser (not your web browser). For simplicity we shall refer to this directory as `moodle/`.

| | |
|---|---|
| **Activity module** | `moodle/mod/` |
| **Assignment type** | `moodle/mod/assignment/type/` |
| **Block** | `moodle/blocks/` |
| **Course format** | `moodle/course/format/` |
| **Filter** | `moodle/filter/` |
| **Integration** | (varies by module, look for additional instructions) |
| **Question type** | `moodle/question/type/` |

Most modules are self contained within a single subdirectory. This is especially true for modules created for more recent versions of Moodle. So, generally, you should be able to unzip the contents of the module package to one place.

Within the `zip` file, there will normally be a structure that should become the directory structure when unzipped. This will usually be a single directory at the root of the `zip` file and subfolders within this. Depending on the complexity of the module, there may be a few PHP files or there may be hundreds of files for images, scripts, language translations, and more.

 Be careful that the folder structure from the `zip` file is maintained when it is extracted.

Unzip the `progress.zip` file inside the `moodle/blocks` directory. The path to the root of the module code should be `moodle/blocks/progress`.

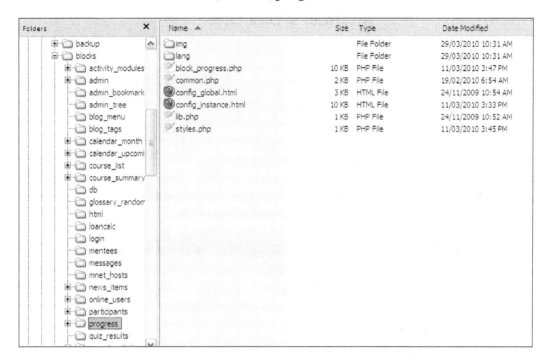

When you unzip the files, be sure that you do not add additional directories, for example `moodle/blocks/progress/progress/`. Doing so will prevent the block code from being detected and installed. Also take care not to accidentally rename the directory or the files within it as this will affect the functioning of the module.

Once the files are in place, the next step is to install the module. For most modules the process is the same.

1. Log in as the system administrator.
2. Go to the root of the site page.
3. Look for the block labeled **Site Administration**.

4. Click on the **Notifications** link.

5. When you click on the **Notifications** link, a scan will be conducted for new modules and updates of existing modules. Database tables will be set up during this process.

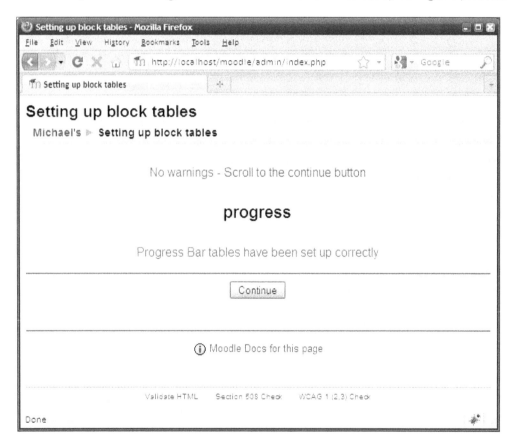

6. Once the module is installed, you can begin using it. To try the Progress Bar block, go to your course and click on **Turn editing on**. On the right-most column at the bottom, there is a block containing a list for adding blocks. Select the block name, for example, **Progress Bar**, to add it.

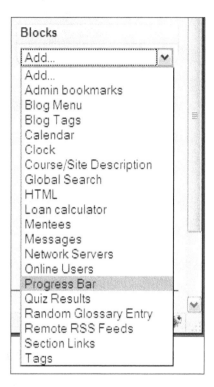

7. After you have added a block you will want to change its settings. With editing turned on, look for the **Update** settings icon on the block. It may vary in appearance when different themes are used, but often it is depicted as a hand holding a pen, or a pen over a notepad:

If you are not sure what the icons on a block do, hover over them for a description. Some blocks will not function properly until you have changed their settings.

When you add an activity module, an assignment type, or an integration, you can add an instance by selecting it from the list of resources or activities, depending on what kind of module it is. When you add a module of this kind you will immediately be taken to a page to set it up.

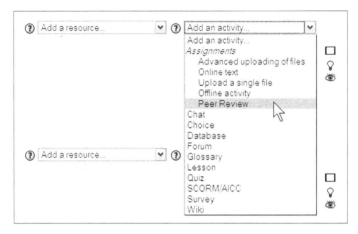

Question types allow a greater variety of questions to be added to quizzes. Once you have copied the directory of files for a question type to `moodle/question/type/`, visit the **Notifications** page as normal. You should then be able to select that question type when creating a new question.

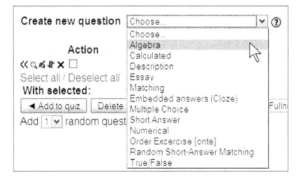

 Knowing how to install a module is useful. Getting the best results from the module when it is used for teaching is more critical. Instructions describing how to set up common modules for practical teaching can be found in the later chapters of this book.

## How it works...

Moodle is designed to be modular, and also to make the process of adding modules as easy as possible. Allowing the code for a module to be in a self contained directory allows module authors to create and share modules without requiring a complicated installation or detailed instructions. Once you've installed one module, installing more is relatively easy.

Not all modules can be contained in a single directory. If this is not the case, you will be provided with additional instructions for installation. A common change needed for some module types is to add a string to a language file. For extra information check the following:

- The **Modules and plugins** database entry for the module
- Moodle documentation pages for the module
- A `readme.txt` file in the `zip` package

## There's more...

Filters and course formats are installed in a slightly different way compared to blocks, activity modules, and question types.

### Filters

Once you have copied the module code to the `moodle/filter/` directory, log in as the administrator and go to the root page of your site. At this stage if you were to visit the **Notifications** page, nothing will be shown as no databases are needed for filters. On the **Site Administration** menu, expand **Modules** and you will see a link to **Filters**. Expanding this will show a link to **Manage Filters**. Clicking this will take you to the filters settings page.

The newly added filter should appear in the list of filters. Clicking the closed-eye icon will enable the filter. Text appearing in labels, web pages, and forums will be filtered and text matching the code specific to the filter will be replaced accordingly. The following is an example of a filter that replaces code, such as `(smile)` with icons.

## Course formats

Course formats allow the layout of a course page to take on a different structure.

To add a course format, copy the format directory and files into the `moodle/course/format/` directory, log into the course, choose **Settings** from the course **Administration** block, then choose your new format from the list of formats.

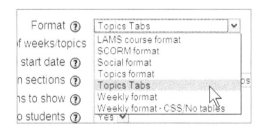

### See also

- ► Changing site-wide settings
- ► Getting rid of modules

# Changing site-wide settings

Activity modules and blocks can have site-wide settings that you can adjust. These settings allow consistent changes in the use of the module across an entire site, but even during testing you might want to change such settings. It may be that you just want to see what settings can be changed globally for a module.

## Getting ready

To achieve this you must have your web server running with Moodle installed. You need to be able to log in as the administrator, or get the help of someone who can. You should have installed the modules that you want to change settings for.

The following steps assume you have installed the Progress Bar block, which has global settings that can be changed.

## How to do it...

Log in as the site administrator and visit the root page of the site. To get to the global settings of a module, on the **Site Administration** menu, select **Modules**, then **Activities** or **Blocks**, whichever is appropriate. The Progress Bar block is a block, so select **Blocks** to reach its global settings.

The next step is to select the name of the module. For our test, the module name is **Progress Bar**. The settings for the module should appear in a form.

Not all activity modules or blocks have global settings. For many modules, this is not necessary. Changes to the global settings affect the configuration of the module, including any instances that may already exist, and any that are added in future, across the site.

## There's more...

Be a little careful when changing global settings on a live site. If the module is currently in use, changing global settings can affect the experience of students and teachers. Accidentally using invalid global settings can detrimentally affect the running of the module on the site.

## See also

▶ Adding modules to Moodle

▶ Getting rid of modules

# Getting modules to speak your language

Another feature of Moodle is its capacity for internationalization. This means that the same software can be used by people speaking different languages. While translations for over 80 languages are available for the core functionality of Moodle, most modules only offer translations for a smaller number of languages, and the language you are teaching in may not be one of them.

Adding a translation for a module is simple to do. If you give your translation to the author of the module, your efforts could also benefit others who speak your language.

## Getting ready

It is assumed that you have set the default language for your site. If not, there is more information about adding a language pack and setting the language for your site later.

In order to create a translation for a module, you don't need any real programming experience; it's actually quite simple. Some understanding of HTML tags can be an advantage.

You will need a text editor that can create and edit Unicode files. Word processors are not appropriate for this task, and a simple editor, such as Windows Notepad, is not up to the job. There are many free editors available that will allow you to create and edit Unicode files. One example available for Windows is Notepad++, which is a free editor and is also available as a portable application.

The steps that follow provide an example that assumes the Progress Bar block has been installed.

## How to do it...

Where the module was installed, there will usually be a `/lang` folder. For the Progress Bar block this is located at `moodle/blocks/progress/lang`. Within this folder, there are folders for different languages, most of them contributed by users around the world.

If you are reading this, it is assumed you have an understanding of English, so have a look inside the `en_utf8/` folder. You will see a file called `block_progress.php` and another directory called `help/`. The `block_progress.php` file contains strings of text used in the module, each with a code and the string displayed on screen. Open this file in your editor to see the contents.

```php
<?php

$string['activity'] = 'activity';
$string['assignment'] = 'Assignment';
$string['assignment_submitted'] = 'submitted';
$string['choice'] = 'Choice';
$string['choice_answered'] = 'answered';
```

Inside the `lang/help/progress/` directory there are a number of HTML files, each relating to a help topic. These appear when a help icon (usually appearing as a question mark) is clicked. Opening these files in your web browser will show you the rendered version of these files and opening them in your editor will show you the HTML source of the documents.

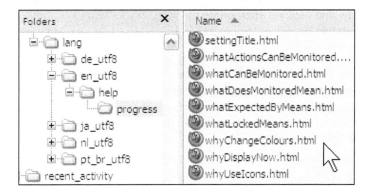

To add a new language, you first need to find out the two letter code for your language. To see the list of supported languages visit the following site. You will also see the code letters for each language, and you need to follow the same code. Refer to `http://download.moodle.org/lang16/`.

Return to the `lang/` folder. For the Progress Bar block this is at `moodle/blocks/progress/lang/`. Assuming that you know English as a second language, copy the `en_utf8/` folder and all of its content. Rename the folder with the two letter code for your language, for example, the folder for Afrikaans would be `af_utf8/`. Be sure to preserve the filenames and folder names within (they do not need translation, only the contents).

Open the `block_progress.php` file in your Unicode editor. You need to translate the string on the right of the = symbol, within the quotes. Do not translate the code value for the string on the left. You may need to see the string in use to get a sense of what the string is intended for, in order to make an accurate translation. If you include any apostrophes within the string, escape the quote with a slash, as shown in the following example, otherwise the string will be seen as coming to an end earlier than it should.

```
$string['owners'] = 'Owner\'s';
```

If there is code within the strings, or HTML tags, that you are unsure about, leave these and just translate any text around them.

You can also translate the HTML files in `moodle/blocks/progress/lang/help/progress/` to produce help files in your language. Open these in your editor and translate the text within the files. Again, avoid changing any HTML or code you don't understand. Some help files also include PHP code segments within `<?php` and `?>` tags, avoid changing this content.

Be sure to test your translated files. If, after changing a translation file, nothing appears on the course page, it may be that you have inadvertently created an error. Typically this comes from mismatched quotes around strings. Be sure each starting quote is matched with a closing quote, and any enclosed quotes are escaped. Test that your translated text items are appearing correctly and have an appropriate meaning in your language. Once created, you can use this translation throughout your site.

The final step is to send your translation to the author of the module. You should be able to find their contact details on the Moodle **Modules and plugins** database entry page for the module. If you have translated the language strings but not translated the help files, this is still a helpful contribution that can be shared. `Zip` up the files you have translated and e-mail them to the author who will usually be more than happy to include your contribution within the module for future downloaders.

## How it works...

Each time the module is loaded, its code is interpreted by the web server and HTML is produced to form the part of the page where the module will appear. Within the code, instead of writing text strings in the author's language, there are calls to functions that check the language and draw the appropriate strings from the language files. This way, all that is needed to change from one language to another is a different language file.

## There's more...

If you want to use another language throughout your Moodle site, the following sections are a basic guide for installing and selecting the language.

## Adding a language pack

Visit the following site to find if a language pack is available for your language:
`http://download.moodle.org/lang16/`.

If your language is available, download the appropriate `zip` file and extract its contents to the directory `moodle/lang/`. If your language is Afrikaans, for example, the language files should be contained in `moodle/lang/af_utf8/`. Ensure you do not introduce additional unnecessary directory levels.

## Selecting a language for your site and courses

A language can be set as a default for courses on the site. This can be overridden at the course level if desired, or by students individually.

To set the default language, log in as administrator and go to the site root page. On the **Site Administration** menu, select **Language**, then **Language Settings**. The default language can be set on the page that appears.

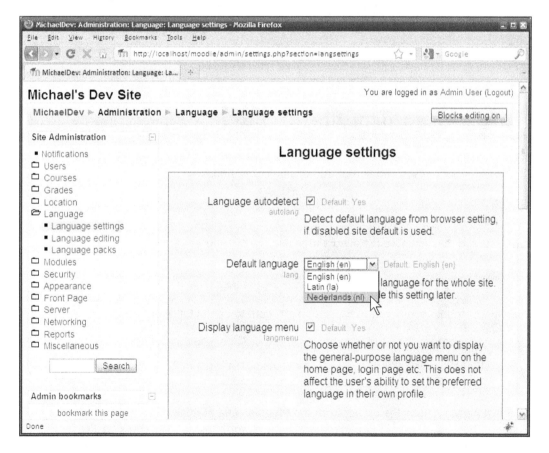

Individual users can set a preferred language in their profile settings.

For individual courses a language can be set. This will "force" students to use that particular language rather than their preferred language.

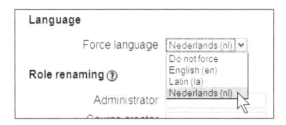

## See also

▶ If it's not quite what you want...

# If it's not quite what you want...

You may have found a module that is helpful, but not exactly what you want. There are a number of ways that you can contribute to changes in modules.

## Getting ready

It is assumed that you have installed and tested the module you are interested in.

## How to do it...

You can contribute in different ways. You might want to do the following:

▶ Thank the author and let them know you are interested in their module

▶ Request a new feature

▶ Report a bug

The best place to thank the author is on the **Modules and plugins** database entry for the module. That way others will see that the module is worth testing. You can also give a rating for the module there.

To request a new feature, the best way is to e-mail the author of the module. Authors are not notified of postings on their **Modules and plugins** entry page, they only see these postings if they check manually. If there is a forum thread for the module, that can also be a good place to contribute ideas for changes. The authors will usually be subscribed to such forums, particularly if they have posted to the forum themselves.

If you find a bug in a module, try to find a method to reproduce the bug. Consider if the bug is something that might only happen on your server for some reason. If you're confident that you have found a bug that needs fixing, create a "new issue" on the Moodle Tracker at this URL: `http://tracker.moodle.org/secure/Dashboard.jspa`. You will need to create an account. The tracker supports bug resolution and communication between you and the author.

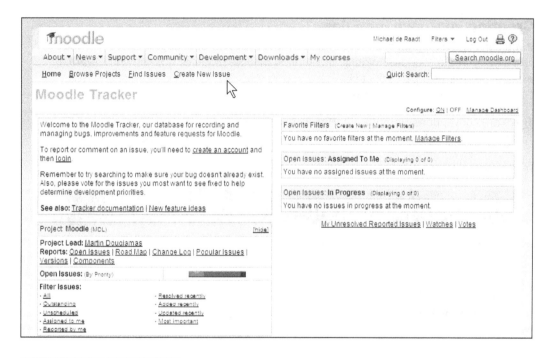

## How it works...

Moodle is all about learning and sharing. The people who create contributed modules are often teachers themselves, or people interested in open source software. Please allow time for bugs to be fixed and don't be surprised if the author rejects your feature suggestion. It's really 'their baby'.

Module authors have 'opened up' their source. Within reason, you are free to make changes to the modules so that they suit your needs and possibly the needs of others at your institution. If this is what you want to do, read on.

## There's more...

Because the source of modules is made available, you are able to make changes yourself, or to ask other, possibly more technically minded people, to do so for you.

If you do make changes, you need to be willing to share the source code you write with others, and stick to the GNU license conditions. More information is available on the following two pages:

`http://docs.moodle.org/en/About_Moodle`

`http://docs.moodle.org/en/License`

### Creating your own modules

If you can't find a module to suit your needs in the **Modules and plugins** database, you can always create your own. Writing and sharing Moodle modules is a rich and rewarding experience. The best part about sharing modules you have written is knowing that your code will be used around the world. The idea you have may also help many others.

There are conventions, libraries, interfaces, and processes that need to be learned. To get started, visit this URL: `http://docs.moodle.org/en/Development`.

Sometimes, the best way to see how it's done is to look at other authors' code.

# Getting rid of modules

So you gave that module a go and it wasn't what you wanted. How can you get rid of it?

## Getting ready

It is assumed you have your web server running, you have installed a module and now you want to say goodbye to it.

## How to do it...

Activity modules (and usually integrations) and blocks can be deleted in two steps.

- ▶ For activity modules, visit the **Activities** management page (**Site Administration | Modules | Activities | Manage Activities**). Click on **Delete** to remove all instances of the module in courses and any tables set up for the module.

- For blocks, visit the **Blocks** management page (**Site Administration | Modules | Blocks | Manage Blocks**). Click on **Delete** to remove all instances of the block and any tables set up for the block module.

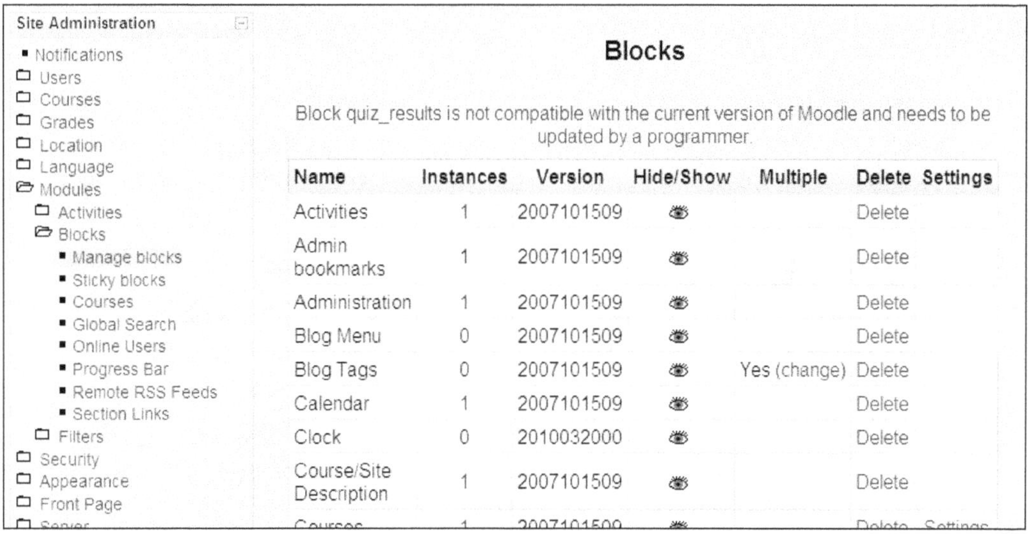

| Site Administration | | | | | | | |
|---|---|---|---|---|---|---|---|
| • Notifications | | | | | | | |
| ▢ Users | | | | | | | |
| ▢ Courses | | | | | | | |
| ▢ Grades | | | | | | | |
| ▢ Location | | | | | | | |
| ▢ Language | | | | | | | |
| ⊟ Modules | | | | | | | |

**Blocks**

Block quiz_results is not compatible with the current version of Moodle and needs to be updated by a programmer.

| Name | Instances | Version | Hide/Show | Multiple | Delete | Settings |
|---|---|---|---|---|---|---|
| Activities | 1 | 2007101509 | 👁 | | Delete | |
| Admin bookmarks | 1 | 2007101509 | 👁 | | Delete | |
| Administration | 1 | 2007101509 | 👁 | | Delete | |
| Blog Menu | 0 | 2007101509 | 👁 | | Delete | |
| Blog Tags | 0 | 2007101509 | 👁 | Yes (change) | Delete | |
| Calendar | 1 | 2007101509 | 👁 | | Delete | |
| Clock | 0 | 2010032000 | 👁 | | Delete | |
| Course/Site Description | 1 | 2007101509 | 👁 | | Delete | |
| Courses | 1 | 2007101509 | 👁 | | Delete | Settings |

(Left navigation menu within the image:)
- Activities
- Blocks
  - Manage blocks
  - Sticky blocks
  - Courses
  - Global Search
  - Online Users
  - Progress Bar
  - Remote RSS Feeds
  - Section Links
- Filters
- Security
- Appearance
- Front Page
- Server

After deleting activity modules and blocks using the **Site Administration** interface, you still need to delete the code for these modules. If you don't remove the code, the module will be re-installed the next time you visit the **Notifications** page.

## How it works...

As Moodle is modular and relies on many contributed modules to allow flexibility, the means of removing modules needs to be just as simple as adding them. With activity modules and blocks, that is the case. This covers most modules you will want to add. For other types of modules, removal is not so simple. To find out more, read on.

## There's more...

Filters, course formats, assignment types, and question types need to be removed in special ways.

### Removing filters

To remove a filter, first visit the **Filters** page (**Site Administration | Modules | Filters | Manage Filters**) and disable the filter (click on the eye icon). You are then free to remove the files for the filter from `moodle/filter/` directory.

## Removing course formats

To remove a course format, simply remove its directory from `moodle/course/format/`. If the format was in use and is no longer available, the format will revert back to a default. It might be wise to check which courses are using the format and set the format for those courses to an acceptable alternative before removing the course format.

## Removing assignment types and question types

Unfortunately there is no clean way to remove an assignment type. It's an activity, but it's not an activity module that appears in the list of activities in the **Site Administration** section. Question types are also somewhat problematic to remove.

If the assignment type or question type is no longer needed, follow these steps.

1. If you have a live site that services teachers and students, put the site in **Maintenance mode** (**Site Administration | Server | Maintenance mode**).

2. Remove all instances of the assignment type or question type from courses.

3. Manually remove the tables related to the module from the database. Take care not to remove other tables such as the 'assignment submissions table' which is used generally. If you are not sure about which tables to remove, don't remove any.

4. Remove the source code.

5. Take the site out of **Maintenance mode**.

# Allowing modules to access outside information

Some modules require access to information outside your server. To achieve this, some modules use the cURL PHP library. If PHP is installed, the cURL library is likely to be available with your web server, but it may be disabled. The XAMPP server has cURL disabled by default.

## Getting ready

To enable cURL in PHP 5 on XAMPP, you need to edit the `php.ini` file. This file is located in the `php\` directory under your web server's root directory.

## How to do it...

Within the file, locate the following line:

```
;extension=php_curl.dll
```

Remove the semi-colon to uncomment this line. This will enable the cURL library. Save the file after making this change. Restart the Apache server for this to take effect.

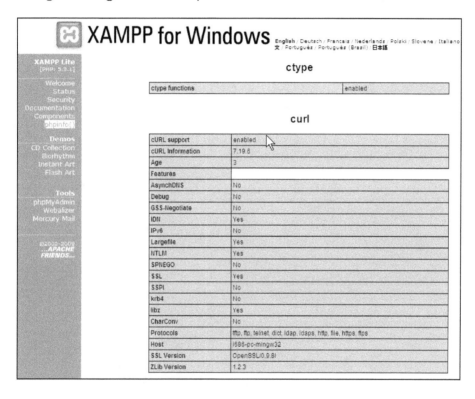

If you visit the **phpinfo** page, cURL support should be enabled.

Even with cURL enabled, you may still have problems if your site is hosted behind a firewall. If this is the case, contact your network administrator.

# 2
# Adding Content

In this chapter, we will cover:

- ▶ Adding video
- ▶ Creating image slideshows
- ▶ Working with books
- ▶ Visualizing programs
- ▶ Looking for a map?
- ▶ Writing mathematical formulae using drag-and-drop

## Introduction

Perhaps the most obvious use of a Learning Management System is to distribute content to students. This chapter looks at modules that allow content to be added to Moodle in new and exciting ways.

 With each module introduced it is assumed that you will know how to locate, download, and install the module. Any unusual installation details will be described for each module, but the focus from this chapter onwards is on how to set up and use the module once it is installed.

## Adding video

With faster connection speeds and greater storage potential, distributing course content in video form is becoming more feasible than ever before.

Video editing software often allows you to export to Flash format and may even provide you with an HTML wrapper for your video. Videos can also be hosted using services such as YouTube. You may have found a public video on a hosting site that you want to share with students.

It is possible to link to video content without adding modules, but this takes the videos out of the context of the course content. Trying to embed videos into web pages requires a knowledge of HTML and the different tags that will work with different browsers. The following activities come to the rescue; assisting you to embed videos in your course. They are described in the later sections of this chapter.

- emboodle
- Flash Video
- YouTube Video Playlist
- MultiVideo Filter

## Creating image slideshows

Want to share your holiday snaps with your course? How about those pictures of the Icelandic volcano erupting, or the works of a famous artist? In many courses there is a need to show an array of images to students. While it is possible to create web pages that include images, writing such pages can be tedious and later they are awkward to update. There are a couple of modules that can make displaying images much simpler, but one stands out.

- Lightbox Gallery

## Working with books

The Book module brings web pages closer to a real textbook. It allows teachers to present course materials in a structured fashion—with chapters, sub-chapters, and a table of contents. There are also blocks written to work with the Book module that extend books to the course page.

- Book module
- Search Books block
- Random Content block

## Visualizing programs

Teaching programming is an unrelenting struggle, battling the forces of injustice where ever they may appear. Well, actually it is quite rewarding and sometimes even enjoyable. But trying to bring interactive examples into materials is difficult indeed, and there are few Moodle modules able to help in this task. But if you are teaching Java, there is one module that you might find very useful.

  ▸   Jeliot

## Looking for a map?

Imagine viewing the world from the heavens, with a bird's-eye-view from country to country and into everyone's back yard. Imagine the potential educational possibilities such power could bring. Well imagine no more.

  ▸   Map module

## Writing mathematical formulae using drag-and-drop

Creating material with mathematical formula either requires an understanding of TeX syntax, or a good friend down the hall who knows TeX. But now there is a module that can help you drag-and-drop your equations together.

  ▸   DragMath Equation editor

# Adding video pages

| Name | emboodle |
|---|---|
| Module type | Activity |
| Author | John Booker |
| Released | 2009 |
| Maintained | Little activity |
| Languages | English |
| Compliance | Good (There's not much to it) |
| Documentation | No help files or online documentation |
| Errors | None displayed |

This is a very simple module for embedding video content hosted on sites like YouTube. If you have emboodle installed, and you can find the page you want on YouTube, this module will take care of the rest.

## Getting ready

Download and install the emboodle module into the `/moodle/mod/` directory and visit the **Notifications** page.

## How to do it...

Before adding an emboodle activity, find your source video page on the video hosting site. Copy the address of the page. A simple way to do this is to copy the text in the address bar at the top of the page. Keep this address in the 'clipboard' to be pasted later.

In your course page, add emboodle from the **Add an activity** list. The following configuration page should appear:

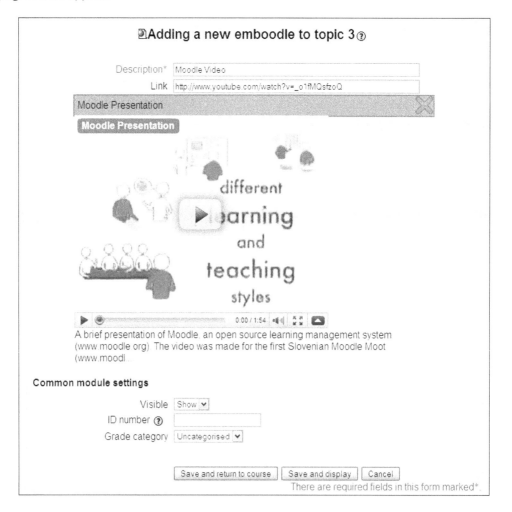

Setting up an emboodle activity is truly simple. Apart from the common module settings, there are only two specific settings needed. The first is a description, which becomes a link to the embedded video's source page.

The second setting is the address of the page where the video was found. Paste the address of the source page for the video here. With this information in place the module goes into action, attempting to detect the necessary information for the video. If found, it displays a preview of the video on the configuration page. This search must make a number of different attempts. At first it may report failure, but without any intervention it should continue searching for information and eventually find what it needs.

The title of the video (which becomes the **Link** text on your course page) and a description are automatically gathered from the video's source page.

## How it works...

When added, an emboodle activity is very simple. It has a wrapper for the Flash video with player controls including a play-pause button, a timeline and time information, volume control, full-screen button, and an options button. Above the video is a link to the source page for the video. Next to the video is a description gathered from the source page.

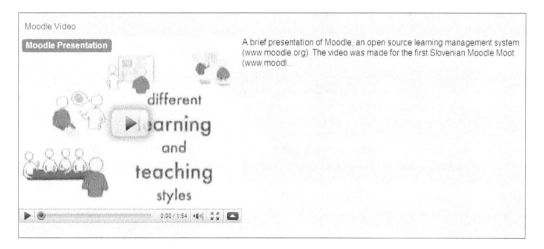

## There's more...

The emboodle plugin uses oohEmbed which facilitates all kinds of embeddable content, not just video. For example you can embed pictures from Flickr.

See oohEmbed for details of supported providers.

## See also

▶ Flash video activity

# Adding a Flash Video

| Name | Flash Video |
|---|---|
| **Module type** | Activity |
| **Author** | Rashan Anushka |
| **Released** | 2007 |
| **Maintained** | Actively, but not so much recently |
| **Languages** | English |
| **Compliance** | Good |
| **Documentation** | No help files or online documentation |
| **Errors** | None displayed |

The Multimedia filter, when turned on, allows you to insert players for media files in locations around your course, however, this filter does not allow such multi-media content to be the focus of an activity.

The Flash Video module allows you to create pages containing your own Flash video files. You can add information about the video above the video itself. You can also add notes on a separate tab and students can add their notes individually.

You may be hesitant to try this activity because it suggests third party software is necessary, and no documentation was provided for download location, installation or why this extra software was even needed. If you have large Flash video files and lots of them, it may be prudent to install the recommended Red5 video streaming server, although even if you can find it, the documentation for this is not very helpful.

It turns out, though, that you can upload and embed Flash files using the Flash Video Activity module without a streaming server. So if you have only small videos, this should be sufficient.

## Getting ready

Download and install the Flash Video module into the `/moodle/mod/` directory and visit the **Notifications** page.

## How to do it...

In your course page, add Flash Video from the **Add an activity** list. The following configuration page should appear.

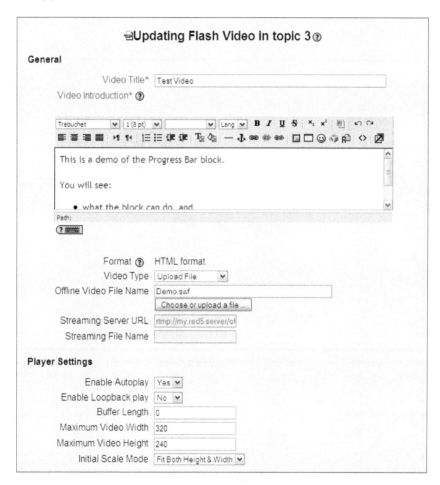

You need to provide a title and some introductory text for the video. This introductory text is where you would place written material that complements the video. This allows you to present the materials in more than one modality. There are also settings to control how the video is played and the size it appears on the page. These are passed onto the Flash wrapper/player that controls the video.

When the video is shown it is presented with controls including a play-pause button, a timeline, time information, and a volume control. The button to maximize the video to full-screen did not seem to work during testing.

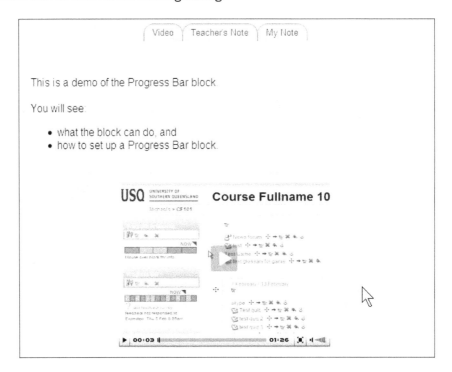

To add notes, the teacher must click on the **Teacher's Note** tab and then the **Edit the Note** button on the top right.

## There's more...

Here are some practical applications for the Flash Video module:

- ▸ Live welcome messages
- ▸ Recorded lectures
- ▸ Captured desktop demonstrations

## See also

- ▸ emboodle
- ▸ Multimedia Plugins filter (standard in Moodle)

# Creating video blocks

| | |
|---|---|
| **Name** | YouTube Video Playlist |
| **Module type** | Block |
| **Author** | Paul Holden |
| **Released** | 2007 |
| **Maintained** | Could do with updating for recent versions |
| **Languages** | English, (plus language packs for Italian, Portuguese Brazilian, Spanish) |
| **Compliance** | Good |
| **Documentation** | Limited online documentation |
| **Errors** | Errors displayed with all error reporting turned on |

The YouTube Video Playlist block allows you to build a list of YouTube videos from which it will select a single video when the block is displayed.

## Getting ready

Download and install the block directory into the `/moodle/blocks/` directory and visit the **Notifications** page.

You will need to have found a video hosted on YouTube and know the address of the page that shows the video.

## How to do it...

Once installed, the block can be configured by visiting the block's configuration page.

This block expects you to create a playlist of videos available from YouTube. Once you have found a video at YouTube that you would like to add, copy the URL of the page from the address bar. Go to the configuration page for the block and click on the **Add/Edit Video** tab at the top of the page. Enter a **Title** and **Description** and paste the URL of the page that contained the video on YouTube. The **Shared** option indicates whether or not you wish to share the block with other courses. If you wish to change any of these details after they are saved, you can do so from the **Manage Videos** tab.

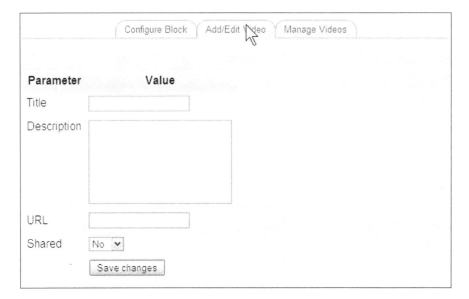

Once you have added details for a video, you are taken to the **Configure Block** tab. It is here that you can build and adjust the playlist of videos. Newly added videos appear in the **Available Videos** list. If you wish them to be a candidate for display when the block is loaded, select the videos and use the left arrow button to transfer the video to the **Playlist**.

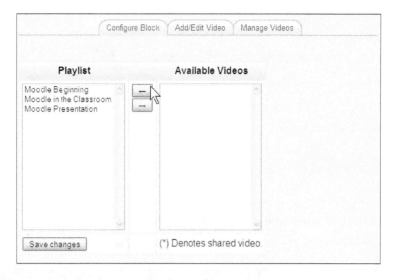

## How it works...

A single video is selected from the playlist and shown in the block when the course page is loaded. A different video is selected at each reload, but it is not clear if this is random or based on some order.

The block width pushes outwards to greater than the normal width, and there is no setting to control this.

## There's more...

Here are some practical applications for video in blocks:

- ▶ Short, snappy welcome messages, right on the course page
- ▶ Guided tours of the course page
- ▶ Reminders for upcoming activities

## See also

- ▶ MultiMovie Filter
- ▶ MultiMovie Block (see **Modules and plugins** database)
- ▶ INWICAST MediaCentre (see **Modules and plugins** database)

# Adding videos anywhere

| | |
|---|---|
| **Name** | MultiMovie Filter |
| **Module type** | Filter |
| **Author** | Eloy Lafuente (stronk7) |
| **Released** | 2006 |
| **Maintained** | Not much activity recently |
| **Languages** | Not applicable |
| **Compliance** | Good |
| **Documentation** | Limited (`readme.txt` file) |
| **Errors** | None displayed |

If you have sound and video files on your server, the Multimedia Plugins Filter can support a number of multimedia formats.

If you are looking for a simple way to embed videos hosted on YouTube, Google Videos, or TeacherTube around your site, the MultiMovie Filter may be a candidate for you.

## Getting ready

Download and install the MultiMovie Filter into the `/moodle/filter/` directory. Enable the filter at **Site Administration | Modules | Filters | Manage filters**.

You will need to have found a video hosted on YouTube, Google Videos, or TeacherTube and know the address of the page that shows the video.

## How to do it...

When the filter is enabled, coded entries can be written into labels, forum posts, web pages, and descriptions elsewhere around your Moodle site.

The MultiMovie Filter uses the following syntax to embed videos in your site.

```
[[mm:source:reference|video title]]
```

The source is either YouTube, Google or TeacherTube, depending on which of these three sites you find your video. The reference is usually given at the end of the address of the page where the video is found. Be careful copying this over, YouTube codes often begin with an underscore. The video title can be any text you wish to add to describe the video, but be brief; there is only limited space where the title appears.

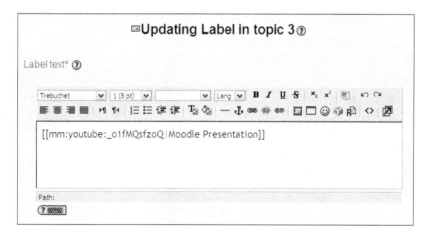

The preceding example shows a MultiMovie filter code being entered in a label for a course page. This is entered as normal text, not as HTML source text.

## How it works...

When your page is being rendered, the text is passed through the filters (that are enabled). If the text matches the filter, such as the preceding syntax, it is replaced by the HTML required to embed that video in your page.

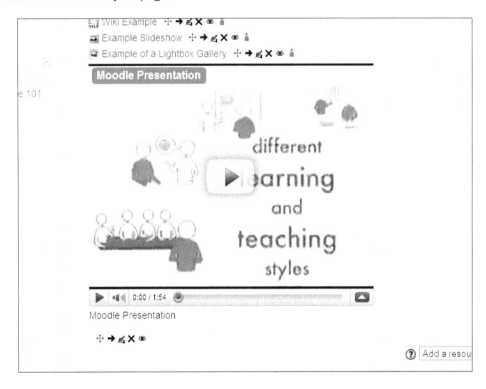

The preceding image shows a label that contains a MultiMovie entry that has been replaced with an embedded video.

## There's more...

Here are some practical applications for the MultiMovie Filter:

▶ Student's favorite YouTube videos in forum posts

▶ TeacherTube videos right in the course page

▶ Use of videos in assignment instructions

## See also

- ▶ emboodle
- ▶ Flash video activity
- ▶ MultiMovie Block (see **Modules and plugins** database)

# Sharing image galleries

| | |
|---|---|
| **Module name** | Lightbox Gallery |
| **Module type** | Resource |
| **Author** | Paul Holden |
| **Released** | 2007 |
| **Maintained** | Actively |
| **Languages** | English, (plus language packs for Basque, Catalan, French, German, Hebrew, Hungarian, Italian, Japanese, Portuguese Brazilian, Spanish) |
| **Compliance** | Good |
| **Documentation** | Limited online documentation |
| **Errors** | None |

If you are wanting to display a library of images to students in a course, here is a solution for you.

The Lightbox Gallery allows a directory of images to be displayed and adds a number of image editing features that may be valuable to teachers.

## Getting ready

Download and install the module into the `/moodle/mod/` directory and visit the **Notifications** page. Check global settings, but avoid diverging from defaults unless you have a specific reason.

## How to do it...

The Lightbox Gallery reads images out of a directory, so before you add it, you will have to create a directory and upload images to it.

Click on **Files** in the **Administration** block on your course page. You will be taken to the files area for your course.

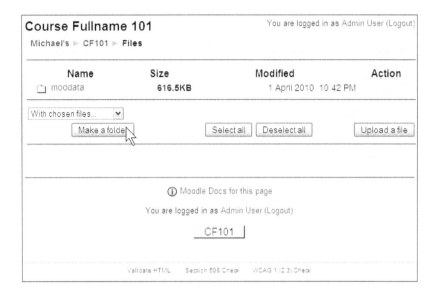

On the left of the files area, near the bottom, click on the button labeled **Make a folder**.

Type in an appropriate name for your folder and click on the **Create** button.

Your new folder should now appear in the files area. Click on the name of the folder to view the folder.

When inside the folder, click the **Upload a file** button. You will be shown a page where you can browse for a file on your computer and upload it. Do this for each image you wish to add to your slideshow. You will want to upload JPEG images (files with a .jpg extension).

On your course page, add a **Lightbox Gallery** from the **Add a resource...** menu.

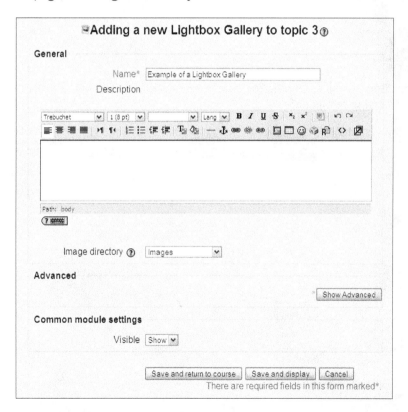

The configuration of a Lightbox Gallery is very simple indeed. All you have to do is name it and select the directory where images are (or will be) stored. You can add a description and there are some advanced settings that can be changed, although the defaults should suit most users.

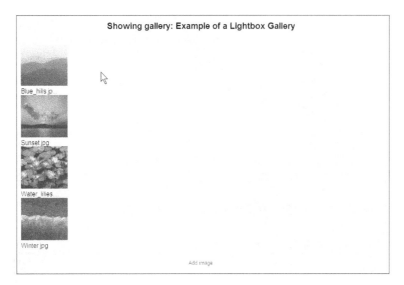

The Lightbox Gallery displays images as thumbnails. When a thumbnail is clicked the image is displayed 'floating' on the page.

With the image displayed a user can navigate forward or backward. Controls for this appear when the user moves the mouse over the top-right or top-left corners of the image respectively. Image information is displayed at the bottom. The user can close this display and return to the thumbnails.

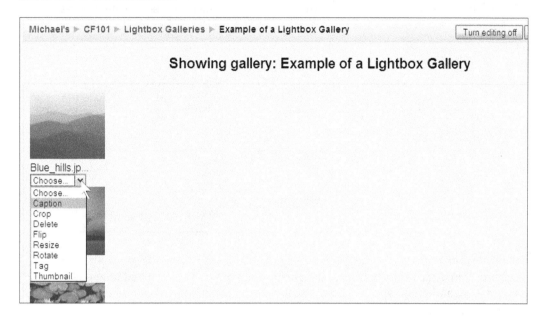

To edit the image and its entry in the gallery, there is a button near the top-right of the page labeled **Turn editing on**. When clicked, the view for the teacher changes and below each image thumbnail there appears a list of properties that can be changed and actions that can alter the image. Clicking one of these takes the teacher to a new page where this can be achieved.

While editing one aspect of the image the teacher can also change other aspects or perform actions on the image by selecting the appropriate tab at the top of the page. This is quite convenient and makes good use of the PHP image libraries. It is also convenient to be able to move forward and backward through the image library, or to jump to another image by selecting its filename from the drop-down list. When changes have been made, the teacher can return to the gallery by clicking the button on the top-right of the page.

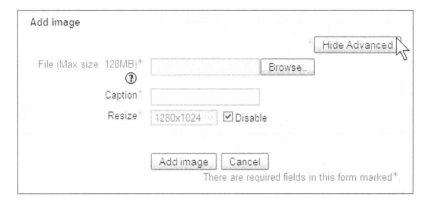

A handy feature of the Lightbox Gallery is the potential to add a new image, or a zipped collection of images. At the bottom of the gallery page is a link labeled **Add image** which leads to a page where image files can be uploaded. You can label and resize images as they are uploaded.

## There's more...

Here are some practical applications for image slideshows:

- ▶ Happy snaps from the class excursion or sports carnival
- ▶ Collected media images of a current news event
- ▶ Historical photos that provide a history of a contemporary topic

# Working with books

| Module name | Book | Search Books | Random Content |
|---|---|---|---|
| Module type | Activity | Block | Block |
| Author | Petr Skoda | Eloy Lafuente (stronk7) and Antonio Vicent | Borja Rubio Reyes |
| Released | 2006 | 2007 | 2008 |
| Maintained | Actively | Actively | Little Activity |
| Languages | Belarusian, Catalan, Czech, Dutch, English, Finnish, French, German, Indonesian, Italian, Japanese, Polish, Portuguese Brazilian, Slovak, Slovenian, Spanish, Swedish | English, Spanish | English, Spanish |
| Compliance | Good | Good | Minimal |
| Documentation | Excellent help files and online documentation | None (but there's not much to it) | None |
| Errors | None | None | Errors displayed with all error reporting turned on |

The Book module is a very popular and useful module that allows course materials to be presented in a more complex and structured way than simple web pages.

There are also a couple of blocks that can be used with the Book module. The Search Books block allows students to search for keywords in a book and be directed to the chapter of the book that contains the keywords. The Random Content block randomly picks a number of chapter titles to tempt students into reading those chapters.

## Getting ready

Download and install the Book module into the /moodle/mod/ directory and visit the **Notifications** page. After installing the Book module you might wish to install the Search Books and Random Content blocks. These can be installed by copying their directories to the /moodle/blocks/ directory then visiting the **Notifications** page.

## How to do it...

Add a **Book** from the **Add a resource...** menu on your course page. The main settings are configured first, the content is added later.

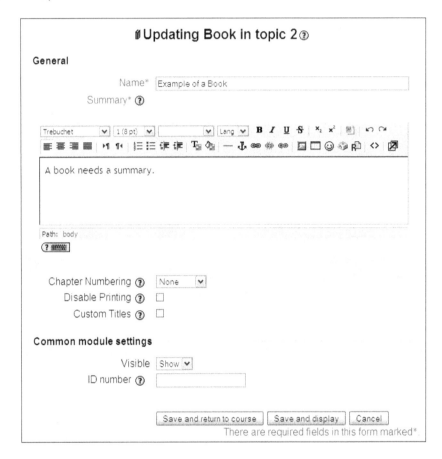

Enter a **Name** and **Summary** for the book. Additional settings can be left at their default values.

When you click the button labeled **Save and display** you will be asked to create the first chapter for your book, as a book requires at least one chapter.

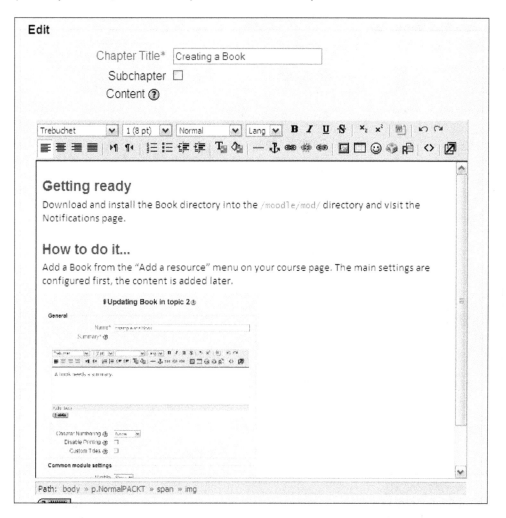

Once you have added a chapter title and content for the chapter, save the chapter and you will be taken to the teacher's view of the book.

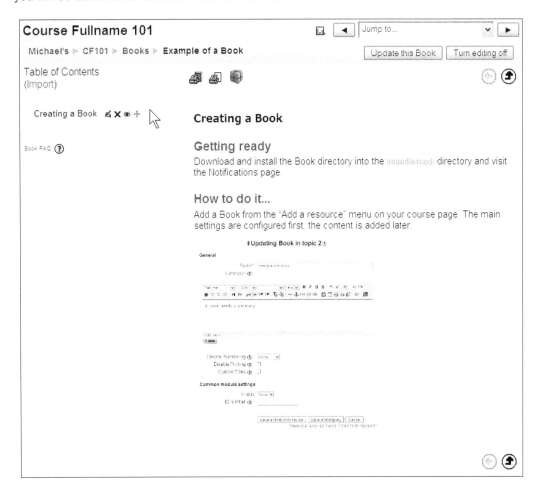

In the table of contents, you can edit, delete, and hide chapters. You can also add more chapters by clicking the red plus symbol. When more than one chapter has been created, you can reorder the chapters using up and down arrows:

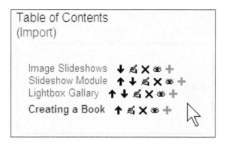

After installing the Book module and setting up one or more books, you can add a Random Content block to tempt students into reading content from one of your books. The block authors suggest this might be useful for books containing FAQs (Frequently Asked Questions) or tips rather than regular course material.

Once you have added the Random Content Block, click the configuration icon to be taken to the block's configuration page.

**Configuring a Random content block**

Book's name:   Example of a Book ▾

Items to show:   3 ▾

Block title:   [                                    ]

Save changes

You must select the title of one of your books. The number of randomly displayed chapter titles can be configured. The block can be given a title, or if left blank the block will take on the book name as its title.

When book content has been added, the content of the book can only be read or printed. Books can be printed in their entirety or by chapter.

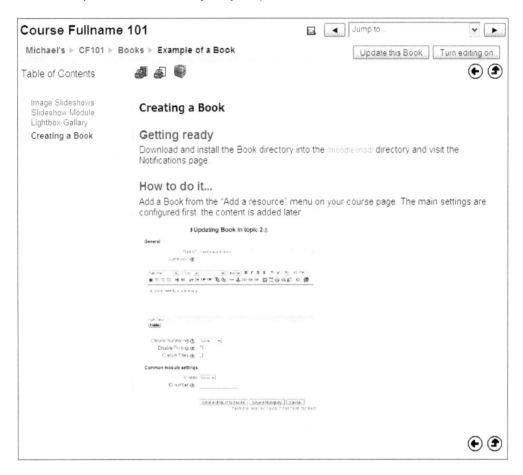

With the Search Books block installed, students can search for keywords in books.

The block then opens a page containing a list of books and chapters that contain the search keywords. The user can follow the links to the book chapter and see the content there.

**Course Fullname 101**

Michael's ▶ CF101 ▶ **Search Book Results**

| download | Search Books |

Results **1** - **2** of about **2** for **"download"**

- Example of a Book » Image Slideshows
- Example of a Book » Creating a Book

The Random Content block searches for book chapter titles from the book set in the block's configuration and randomly shows up to the specified number. Clicking on the chapter name takes the student to that chapter in the book. The student can also click **Show others ...** which reloads the page with a new set of random chapters.

## There's more...

Here are some practical applications for the Book module:

- ▶ Regular course materials (imagine that)
- ▶ A scrapbook of past assignment attempts
- ▶ FAQs and Top tips

# Showing programming examples in Moodle

| Name | Jeliot |
|---|---|
| **Module type** | Activity |
| **Author** | Andrés Moreno |
| **Released** | 2008 |
| **Maintained** | Limited activity |
| **Languages** | English |
| **Compliance** | Good, requires Java WebStart |
| **Documentation** | None |
| **Errors** | None displayed |

Jeliot is a software visualization tool for novice programmers. If you are teaching programming and Java is your language, then this may be a useful tool for you to illustrate the execution of programs to students.

Jeliot is a Java application and this module is a wrapper for the Jeliot environment. The module launches Jeliot and passes it a source code file for the student to work with.

## Getting ready

Download and install the Jeliot files into the `/moodle/mod/` directory, in a subdirectory called `jeliot` (even if the `zip` file has a different name), and visit the **Notifications** page.

## How to do it...

Add a **Jeliot Activity** from the **Add an activity...** menu on your course page. You will then be asked to configure the activity.

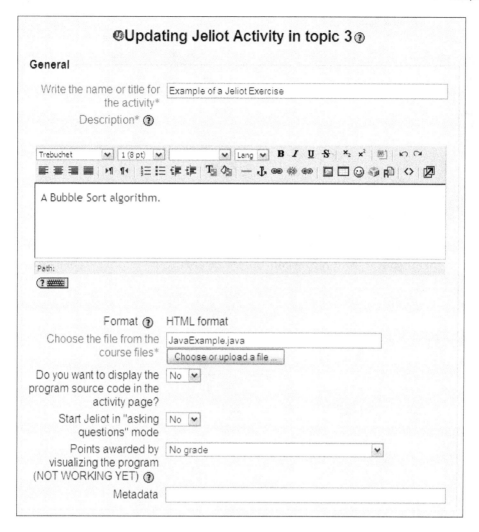

There are three main settings you need to fill in. You will need to add a name and description. You will also need to provide a Java source code file. Clicking on the **Choose or upload a file** button will pop-up a file browser window. In the file browser, you will be able to upload and/or choose a file for this purpose. There are a few other settings that can be changed. These will be sent to the Jeliot application when it is launched. At time of writing it looks as though no feedback can be returned from the application and used for assessment in Moodle.

If you are using this module in your teaching, you will need to ensure that students have the Java Runtime Environment (JRE) installed.

When the activity link is clicked from the course page, it takes a student to a page where they can launch the Jeliot application. Clicking the **Start Jeliot** link causes the browser to download a Java WebStart file, which the student then needs to run with the Java Web Start launcher.

On the first launch, students will be asked to authorize the running of the application and indicate if they trust Java from your server. On successive runs, this check can be bypassed.

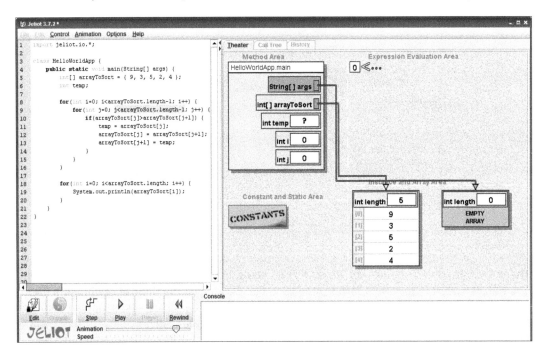

Jeliot shows the application of each statement and the evaluation of each expression. Students can step through the animation, or play the animation at a controlled speed. The visualization maintains a view of each variable and array in memory and simulates the effect of changes to their values.

Jeliot 3 is perhaps not the best available software visualization tool for novice programmers, but it is the only tool with Moodle integration at this stage.

## There's more...

Here are some practical applications for the Jeliot module:

- Algorithm visualization
- Fill-in-the-gap exercises
- Parson's puzzles (jumbled statements with multiple alternatives for each)
- Debugging exercises
- Examples of bad code

## See also

- Jeliot 3 (`http://cs.joensuu.fi/jeliot/index.php`)
- ViLLE (`http://ville.cs.utu.fi/`)

# Getting geographical with the maps

| | |
|---|---|
| **Name** | Map module |
| **Module Type** | Activity |
| **Author** | Ted Bowman |
| **Released** | 2008 |
| **Maintained** | Actively |
| **Languages** | English, Spanish |
| **Compliance** | Good |
| **Documentation** | Online documentation |
| **Errors** | None displayed |

The Map module makes use of online map services from Google Maps, or a combination of OpenStreetMap and OpenLayers. It allows teachers and/or students to add locations with other information to a map. The map can be used to show the locations of students around a country or around the world, or it can be used for a variety of other applications.

## Getting ready

Unlike most other modules, the Map module needs to access information from outside your server. Information about the cURL library and how to enable it, is available in the initial chapter of this book.

It is assumed that you will generally want to use Google Maps unless access is restricted by the Google Maps API terms and conditions.

To access Google Maps from your server you will need an access key and before you can get an access key you will need a Google account. If you don't have one, you will need to set one up.

Download and install the `map/` directory into the `/moodle/mod/` directory and visit the **Notifications** page. After the module's tables are set up, you will be shown the global options for the Map module. In order to use Google Maps, you need to add a key.

At this stage, it would be wise to open a new browser tab and log into your Google account. This will save us running around in authentication circles later. If you don't have a Google account, you might want to set one up now.

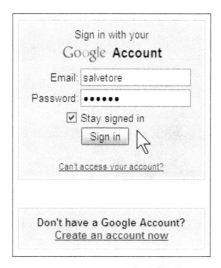

On the Map module's global settings page there is a link to **Find info and obtain API Key here**. Open this link in a new tab so we don't lose track of the Map module's settings page.

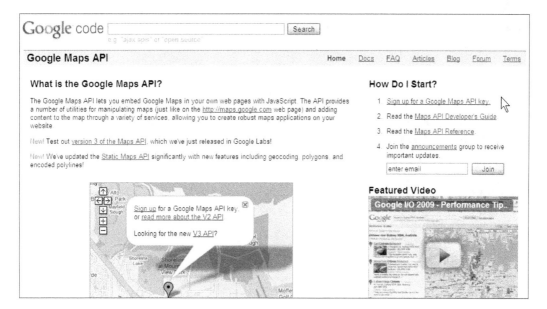

At the top-right of this page under **How Do I Start?** the first link leads you to the start of the key sign-up process.

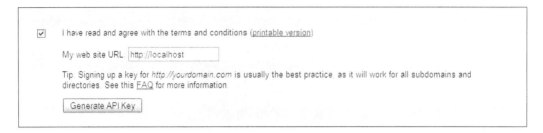

There are a number of conditions associated with applying for a Google Maps API key, and you will want to read these carefully. You need to acknowledge Google's terms and conditions by enabling the tick-box.

Under this is a textbox labeled **My web site URL**. If you are running on a test server, or just around your local LAN, then use `http://localhost`. If you have a site with a registered URL or just an IP address, use that instead.

After this you will be given a key, which is presented in a number of formats. Copy the value of the first to your clipboard:

**General configuration**
(These settings are **always** into effect)

Map Provider: [ Google ▾ ]   Choose which map provider the maps will use.

- Choose on Map - each map created can choose provider
- Google - Find Info and obtain API Key here.
- OpenStreetMaps/OpenLayers

Force Map Provider: [ Yes ▾ ]   If Yes all current maps will use the current provider. If No they will use their current providers.

map_google_api_key: [ ABQIAAAAXp2mBuE7thnybwwPq82e7xT2yXp_ZAY8_ ]   Google MAP Key

Profile State Field: [                              ]   This profile field will be used to determined users' state/province field. You can add a state field to the profiles.

[ Save changes ]

Returning to the Map module's global settings, set the **Map Provider** to **Google**. Set the **Force Map Provider** to **Yes** and paste the Google Maps API key in the appropriate textbox. Click on the button labeled **Save changes**.

## How to do it...

Once the Maps module is installed and the Google Maps API key is set in the module's global settings page, you will be able to set up maps within courses.

Select **Map** from the **Add an activity...** menu and you will be asked to complete settings for this instance of the Map module in your course.

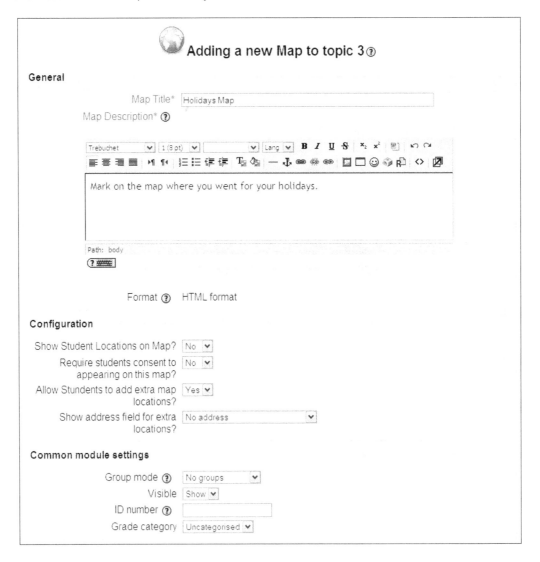

Add a title and description. The title will become the link text on the course page. The description field can be utilized if you are using the map for an activity with students.

Under **Configuration**, the first two settings relate to showing student locations on the map. Student locations are drawn from each student's profile, assuming they are set correctly. Choose **Yes** for the first setting to show student locations. If privacy is a concern, you can require students to volunteer their consent before their location is shown on the map.

For other purposes, for example showing important locations around the world, you will set the first two settings to **No**.

If you wish to allow students to add locations to the map, either to complement locations you have defined or as part of a task set for them, set the third option to **Yes**.

If the granularity of street addresses is needed to differentiate locations, for example marking locations within a single town, changing the final setting to **Addresses only** will allow this. For a finer grain in non-residential areas, co-ordinates can be allowed.

When a Map activity has been added and set up, locations can be added.

Assuming you are identifying important locations for your course, instead of merely showing student locations, you will start off with no locations defined.

You and possibly your students (depending on the settings for the activity), will now be able to add locations to the map. Click on the button labeled **Add an extra location** to add location.

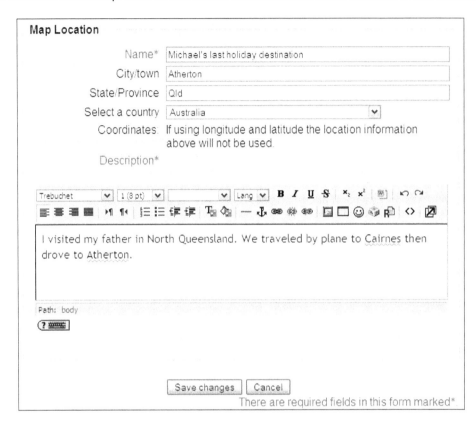

The details for a location can be somewhat incomplete. The Google API does apply some intelligence when finding a location based on the terms provided by a user. The **Name** field is displayed when a user moves the mouse over a location marker. If the location marker is clicked, the **Description** is shown.

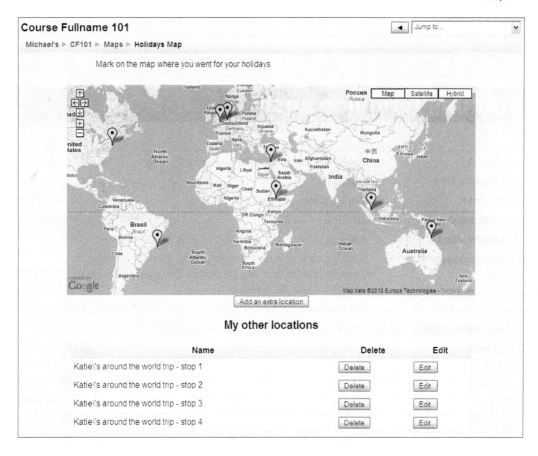

When locations are added to the map, they appear as markers. A user can remove or edit their own location, but not the location of other users. The map can be zoomed and dragged. Satellite images can be overlaid on the map also.

## There's more...

Here are some practical applications for the Map module:

► Countries being studied for geographical, political, or social studies

► Birthplaces of historical persons

► War zones of current and historical battles

► Illustrating travel routes

**See also**

▸ Online Users Google Map block (*Chapter 9, Informing Students*)

# Creating formulae easily

| Name | DragMath Equation editor |
|---|---|
| **Module type** | Integration |
| **Author** | Marc Grober |
| **Released** | 2008 |
| **Maintained** | Actively |
| **Languages** | Catalan, Czech, Dutch, English, Farsi, Finnish, French, German, Italian, Norwegian, Polish, Portuguese Brazilian, Russian, Spanish, Swedish |
| **Compliance** | Not a regular module |
| **Documentation** | Online documentation |
| **Errors** | None displayed (if you can get TeX notation filtering running) |

If you want to include formulae on your site, this can be achieved by turning on the TeX notation filter, which can convert TeX syntax to a rendered image. However, if you are not familiar with TeX and its syntax, this might be a difficult way to create a simple equation. Even if you do know TeX, the syntax can be tricky and erroneous syntax will not be rendered correctly. A tool that can assist in producing syntactically correct notation may be helpful to you.

The DragMath editor is a Java Applet that can be launched from the HTML editor in Moodle. It assists you in creating formulae that can be inserted into labels, web pages, forum posts, and other locations where the HTML editor is used. When the written text is presented in HTML form, the TeX notation is rendered as an image containing the formula in mathematical form.

## Getting ready

Before installing the DragMath editor, you need to turn on the **TeX Notation Filter** at **Site Administration | Modules | Filters | Manage Filters**. In most cases, you do not have a need to alter any of the settings associated with this filter. The Mimetex converter, distributed with Moodle, is capable of transforming most mathematical constructs in TeX. There have been issues with the TeX filter running on later versions of PHP. If you encounter this, you may have to upgrade your Moodle instance.

| Site Administration [-] | Manage filters | | | |
| --- | --- | --- | --- | --- |
| • Notifications | | | | |
| □ Users | | | | |
| □ Courses | **Active filters** | | | |
| □ Grades | | | | |
| □ Location | | | | |
| □ Language | | | | |
| ⊘ Modules | **Name** | **Disable/Enable** | **Up/Down** | **Settings** |
| □ Activities | Skypeicons | 👁 | ↓ | |
| □ Blocks | | | | |
| ⊘ Filters | Multimovie | 👁 | ↑ ↓ | |
| • Manage filters | | | | |
| • TeX Notation | TeX Notation | 👁 | ↑ | Settings |
| □ Security | Database Auto linking | | | |
| □ Appearance | | | | |

As this is an integration instead of a regular module, it is not completely self contained, but there are not too many locations affected. The `zip` file for the editor contains a `lib` directory. This can be copied to `/moodle/` and will copy its content into subfolders of the `lib` directory. This will not overwrite any files, but as the `lib` directory already contains one of the subdirectories, it will ask if it should unzip the files into an existing folder.

Apart from unzipping the files, you also need to make an addition to the file `/moodle/lib/adminlib.php`. In this file, search for the following line, which should be located around line 3200.

```
'insertsmile' => 'em.icon.smile.gif',
```

Below this line, insert the following line. Be sure to include the comma at the end.

```
'insertdragmath' => 'em.icon.dragmath.gif',
```

The addition of this line will cause the DragMath editor icon to appear in the HTML editor beside the emoticons icon.

The DragMath editor is a Java Applet, so the Java Runtime Environment (JRE) needs to be installed on the user's machine.

## How to do it...

Once the DragMath editor is installed and the TeX Notation Filter is enabled, you can add formulae.

Using an HTML editor, enter the text that you want to appear around the formula, then click to place the cursor at the location where you wish to insert a formula.

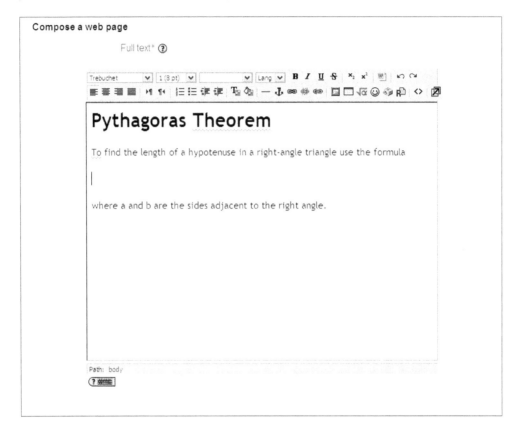

The DragMath editor icon is located next to the emoticon icon and appears as an alpha symbol within a square root. Clicking on the DragMath icon will launch a pop-up window and the DragMath Java Applet will load (assuming the JRE is installed for your browser). You may have to resize this window and if it is the first time using the applet, you will be asked to allow the applet to run.

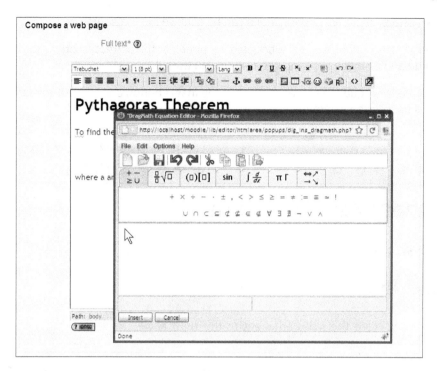

The DragMath editor allows you to include various symbols and constructs in your formula by dragging them into the working area. For example, to include a square root in your formula, click on the second tab, find the icon for a square root and drag this onto the working area.

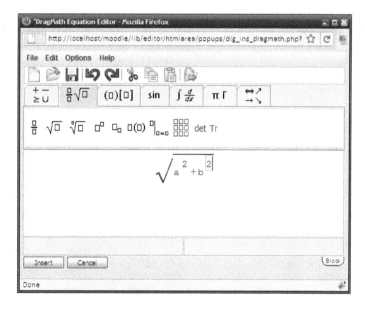

Fractions, powers, integrals, and functions can be achieved in the same way.

Sometimes it can be difficult to get a dragged element into the correct location. You may have to click undo and try again until you get it where you want it.

When you have the equation you want, click on the **Insert** button and the TeX version of your formula will be inserted where the cursor was located.

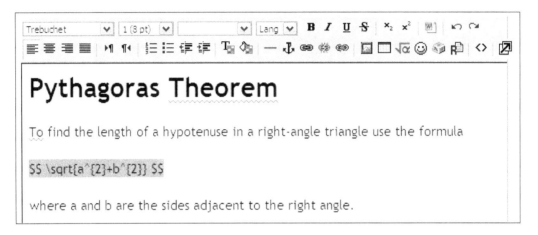

The formula is ready to be filtered by the TeX Notation Filter when this page is rendered.

## How it works...

The text entered in the HTML editor will be passed through each of the enabled filters before it is sent to the user's browser. If the TeX filter encounters text beginning and ending with $$ it knows that the content in between needs to be treated as TeX syntax and rendered as an image.

There are some checks before the conversion is made. If the same string of TeX has been rendered recently, it will reuse the same rendered image instead of re-rendering the TeX again. This is useful if a class of students view the same document containing such a formula, on the same day.

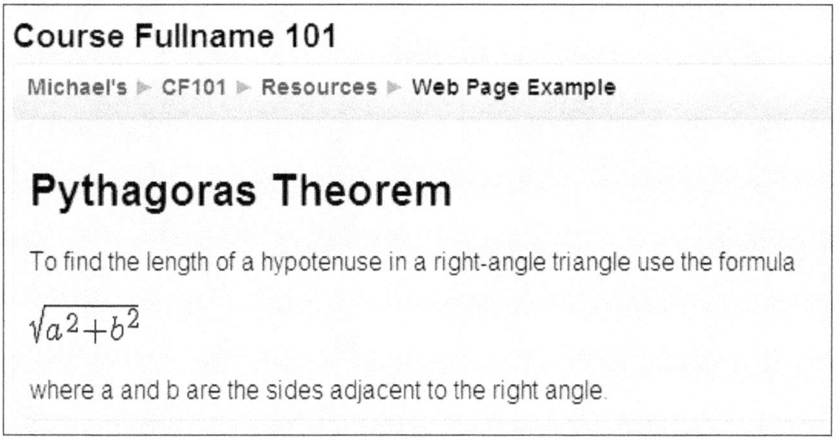

---

## Course Fullname 101

Michael's ▶ CF101 ▶ Resources ▶ Web Page Example

## Pythagoras Theorem

To find the length of a hypotenuse in a right-angle triangle use the formula

$$\sqrt{a^2+b^2}$$

where a and b are the sides adjacent to the right angle.

---

The final product is a mathematical formula, right where you wanted it, and achieved without learning TeX with the aid of the DragMath editor.

## See also

▶ Algebra Filter (standard in Moodle)
▶ jsMath Filter (see **Modules and plugins** database)

# 3

# Connecting to the Outside World

In this chapter, we will cover:

- ▶ Translation blocks
- ▶ Web search in Moodle
- ▶ Accessing Wikipedia
- ▶ Searching for Tweets

## Introduction

It's one thing to put your course materials up on Moodle. But improved education outcomes can be achieved by situating learning in a real-world context. In this chapter, we will look at Moodle modules that can help students be in touch with the world outside.

 In order to access services outside your site, your users will need to have access beyond your local network. You may have to address firewall and security issues before this is possible.

## Translation blocks

Lost for words? The world is now a smaller place and becoming multi-lingual is an expectation for many students. Having tools for translating text may help students with their language-based work.

- ▸ Access Translator Google block
- ▸ Translate block

## Web search in Moodle

Google has become synonymous with searching the web. Bringing Google searches into your course pages can make web searching more convenient and controlled.

- ▸ Moodle Google (Moogle)
- ▸ Google Search block

## Accessing Wikipedia

Wikipedia may not be the best source of information for academic purposes, but for general topics and as a first point of call for projects, it can't be beaten. You can allow students to launch a Wikipedia search from a Moodle course page or direct them to specific Wikipedia entries from within course materials.

- ▸ Wikipedia block
- ▸ Wikipedia filter

## Searching for Tweets

Twitter provides a simple means of social networking. You can also use Twitter in an education setting, or where Moodle is used as the content management system for events (for example, conferences).

- ▸ Twitter Search block

A number of the modules described in this chapter are blocks that include textboxes. While editing is turned on, you might find you cannot add text to such textboxes. You may need to **Turn editing off** before you can test such modules.

# Setting up the Translate Block

| Name | Translate Block |
|------|-----------------|
| **Module type** | Block |
| **Author** | Paul Holden |
| **Released** | 2007 |
| **Maintained** | Actively |
| **Languages** | English, German |
| **Compliance** | Good |
| **Documentation** | Online documentation and `readme.txt` file |
| **Errors** | None |

If you are teaching a language course, or perhaps courses where students need to use more than one language, then having translation tools at hand may be useful for you and your students. The Translate Block is a quick and convenient way to translate text.

## Getting ready

Unzip and copy the Translate Block directory into the `/moodle/blocks/` directory and visit the **Notifications** page.

## How to do it...

As this block includes a textbox, and textboxes may be disabled within blocks while editing is turned on, you may need to **Turn editing off** before you can test it.

Once added to your site, the Translate Block allows you to configure which languages the user can select for translations. It may be desirable to limit languages to those relevant to a course. To do this, access the block's configuration by turning editing on and clicking on the configuration icon on the block.

## How it works...

The Translate Block is quick and convenient. The block uses Ajax to collect the translation and display it in the lower part of the block. For simple phrase translations, this is a very effective tool.

The block is prone to a potential hazard in the form of possible changes to the Google Translate API. During initial testing, this block did not work as the Google API had changed and the downloaded block code had not yet been updated to cater for this change. It was possible to modify the code and feed this change back to the author, and by the time you read this and download the block it should be working. However it may be necessary for the block to be adapted to changes in the Google API in future, and you won't know when the block will need updating until it stops working.

## There's more...

Armed with the Translate Block, you might be looking for uses. Here are some ideas:

- Translating terms in second language classes
- Finding terms common in multiple languages (Sudoku, café, ...)
- Finding crazy translations, possibly when translated phrases are re-translated to their source language
- Translating terms for Moodle module language files

# Allowing Moodle to access Google translator

| | |
|---|---|
| **Name** | Access Translator Google |
| **Module type** | Block |
| **Author** | Jitendra Agrawal |
| **Released** | 2008 |
| **Maintained** | Not actively |
| **Languages** | English (fixed) |
| **Compliance** | Does not allow internationalization. |
| **Documentation** | None |
| **Errors** | None |

The oddly named Access Translator Google block is a simpler block that directs users to a Google Translate page instead of providing the translation within Moodle.

## Getting ready

Take care when downloading the Access Translator Google block; there are two versions on the Moodle **Modules and plugins** database. The earlier version is non-functional with recent Moodle versions, so be sure to get the version added to the database in January 2008. The module is also packaged as a `Tar` file and zipped using `gzip`; if you are using Windows or Mac, you may need an alternate compression program to unpack this module.

Once unpacked, install the block directories into the `/moodle/blocks/` directory and visit the **Notifications** page.

## How to do it...

This block does not try to do anything fancy. There are no settings, no help files and it does not try to capture results and present them within the block using Ajax. This means the block is immune from browser incompatibility problems and changes in the Google Translate API.

The block is not set up for internationalization, which means that if you are not using English, you will need to alter the block code to enter text strings in your language, instead of creating the normal language translation file.

Using the Google logo may mislead students into thinking this is an over-complicated web search block.

The Access Translator Google block allows students to type text they want to translate, and to select the source and target languages.

Clicking the button labeled **Translate** will open a new tab or browser window with their information queried on the Google Translate page.

This is not as convenient as the Translate block, but being simple means this block is also less prone to problems. When the translation services at Google change, this block is likely to live on.

# In-course Web searching with Moogle

| | |
|---|---|
| **Name** | Moodle Google (Moogle) |
| **Module Type** | Block |
| **Author** | Yajuvendrasinh (Yaju) V. Mahida |
| **Released** | 2008 |
| **Maintained** | Actively |
| **Languages** | English |
| **Compliance** | Good |
| **Documentation** | `readme.txt` file, help files do not work |
| **Errors** | Errors displayed with all error reporting turned on |

Bring Google searches into Moodle with this convenient block.

## Getting ready

Install the block into the `/moodle/blocks/` directory and visit the **Notifications** page.

## How to do it...

Once the block is installed, you will be asked to modify global settings for the block. One setting that is critical is the Google Ajax Search API key. This is not the same as the Maps API key if you happen to have that already, but the process is the same.

At the bottom of the block's global configuration page there is a button labeled **Get Google API Key**; when clicked a new tab or browser window will open and you will be taken to the following URL: `http://code.google.com/apis/ajaxsearch/signup.html`.

You will be asked to agree to Google's terms and conditions and supply the URL for your site. If you are running a test server, it is sufficient to use `http://localhost`.

Clicking the button labeled **Generate API Key** will take you to a page having the API key. The value you need is the key by itself at the top of the page. Copy this into the clipboard.

**Thanks for Signing up for a Google AJAX Search API key!**

Your key is:

`ABQIAAAAXp2mBuE7thnybwwPq82e7xT2yXp_ZAY8_ufC3CFXhHIE1NvwkxS08vawHb`

Return to the Moogle block's global settings and paste the API key in the appropriate textbox.

Like other blocks that rely on Google's APIs, this block may be susceptible to changes in the API. When an API changes the block author might update the block. This might not happen immediately, or if the author has moved on, this might not happen at all.

The only other setting you might want to change is the setting to hide the block logo. Although colorful and friendly, this might not fit in with your site.

When the block is added to your course page, it will initially flash a warning indicating that settings for the block need to be set.

Clicking the configuration icon takes you to the configuration page for the block. There are actually a number of pages accessible by clicking the links at the top of the settings page.

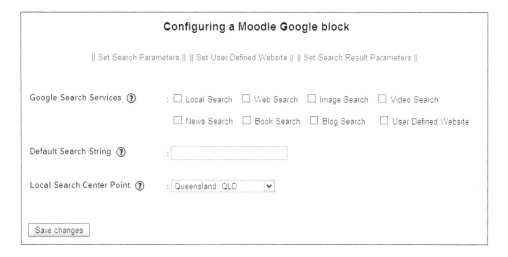

You must select one or more search services by checking the boxes next to each desired service.

The **Local Search** option is unlikely to work with your site unless it is an open site (not requiring authentication).

If a default search string is set, the block will perform a search based on this term each time the block is loaded. This is useful for directing students to specific search results. The block can be used for other searches after this.

If you want students to see search results from content on a designated website, you can add this on the second page of settings labeled **Set User Defined Website**. Here you can add the site URL and a label for the site that will appear as a tab title in the results. If you add a user defined website, be sure to check the box for this on the first page of settings.

# How it works...

When the block is set up, it can complete searches for predefined or user-defined terms. The results are collected and presented in a wonderfully compact tabbed form which doesn't fill the block column.

Users can then expand each tab to see the results of tabs. Web and news search results are presented in simple textual form. Image and video results are given as a series of thumbnails. By default, the results are presented four at a time. The user can see more results by clicking the numbers at the bottom of each list of results.

Instead of taking over the current page, when a link or thumbnail is clicked, a new tab or browser window is opened to view the target page. This is useful if the user is currently working on something in the Moodle page.

## There's more...

You might be wondering what you can do with this block. Here are some ideas:

▸ Direct students to search for links to web pages with contextual information for a project or class topic

▸ Display a list of topical news stories related to a current class topic

▸ Direct students to search within a particular website

▸ Googlewhack (if you are not sure what that means, look it up)

## See also

▸ 'Simple' Google Search block

# Allowing simple Web searches

| Name | 'Simple' Google Search |
|---|---|
| **Module Type** | Block |
| **Author** | Mike Burke |
| **Released** | 2009 |
| **Maintained** | Actively (although there's not much to it) |
| **Languages** | English (fixed in code) |
| **Compliance** | No internationalization |
| **Documentation** | None |
| **Errors** | None |

The 'Simple' Google Search block is a block that allows users to type in terms that will be sent to the Google web search page.

## Getting ready

Install the block into the `/moodle/blocks/` directory and visit the **Notifications** page.

## How to do it...

Once installed, there are no configuration settings and no help files. There is just a textbox used to enter terms which are sent to the Google search engine. Results appear on a new tab or browser window.

If you want to change the behavior or the language for this block, you need to be prepared to edit the block code. The source of the block is contained in a single file called `block_simple_google.php`. Within the file there are lines of HTML that define the appearance of the block when it is rendered on a course page.

```
$this->content->items[] .= "<!-- Google Block By Panic Software-->
<center>

<form action='http://www.google.co.uk/cse' id='cse-search-box'
target='_blank'>
<div>
<input type='hidden' name='cx' value='partner-pub-
6254809892762656:bfrdgi-tjfn' />
<input type='hidden' name='ie' value='ISO-8859-1' />
<input type='text' name='q' size='31' />
<input type='submit' name='sa' value='Search' />
</div>
</form>
<script type='text/javascript' src='http://www.google.co.uk/cse/
brand?form=cse-search-box&amp;lang=en'></script>

</center><!--End of Google Block-->";
```

At present, the block refers all queries to `http://www.google.co.uk/`. You might want to change to your local Google search engine for faster queries and possibly to receive more relevant search results. For a generic solution that works anywhere, replace the current form action attribute `http://www.google.co.uk/cse` with `http://www.google.com/#` and the Google server will redirect you to your local Google server based on your physical location.

The block currently forces a wider than normal width. This is because the text input with name $q$ has a size of 31 characters. This doesn't restrict the number of characters that can be entered, it just sets the width of the textbox. You could reduce this to a smaller number of characters, but a better way to fit the textbox to the block is to remove the size attribute `size='31'` and replace this with a style attribute that will resize the textbox relative to the block `style='width:99%'`.

If you want to change the label of the **Search** button, find the line `<input type='submit' name='sa' value='Search' />` and change the word `Search` to other words, or another language if desired.

If you would like to remove the branding from the textbox, remove the starting and ending `script` tags near the end of this section of code.

 You are within your rights to modify core and contributed Moodle code. However, you should be aware that this comes with some risk. Apart from possible unexpected side effects, once you have changed a module, if you update the module in future, the module code will be overwritten and you will need to re-do any changes you previously made.

While this block is simpler than the Moodle Google block described earlier, it is immune to changes in the Google Search API. While it is less convenient to view search results outside Moodle, users will eventually be viewing pages linked from search results anyway, so perhaps that is not a great inconvenience. What this block lacks is configurability, so it is not as easy to direct students to particular searches.

## See also

▸ Moodle Google block

# Adding Wikipedia search to Moodle

| | |
|---|---|
| **Name** | Wikipedia Block |
| **Module Type** | Block |
| **Author** | David Horat |
| **Released** | 2006 |
| **Maintained** | Actively |
| **Languages** | Chinese, Dutch, English, Finnish, French, German, Greek, Italian, Japanese, Norwegian, Polish, Portuguese, Russian, Spanish, Swedish (for logo image by-line) |
| **Compliance** | Good |
| **Documentation** | `Readme.txt` file |
| **Errors** | None |

This is a simple block that collects a query for Wikipedia and directs the user to a Wikipedia entry in the appropriate language. Languages are determined automatically from the user's language settings.

## Getting ready

Install the Wikipedia Block directory into the `/moodle/blocks/` directory and visit the **Notifications** page. As there are no settings, you won't see the normal message stating tables have been established for the block.

## How to do it...

**Turn editing on** and add the block from the **Blocks** list.

The block should show a logo with a by-line in the user's chosen language, and the language below the search query text box should also default to that language. The preceding screenshot of the block shows what appears when Dutch is the user's preferred language. The language drop-down list below the search block can be changed to see Wikipedia entries in different languages. The default for unknown languages is English.

When the button labeled with a "**>**" is clicked, the query is passed to Wikipedia and the resulting entry should be in the selected language.

By default, Wikipedia entries appear in the current tab or browser window, displacing the Moodle page. You might want to change this so entries appear in a new tab or browser window. Unfortunately there is no setting for this (or anything else about the block) so in order to make this change, you have to delve into the block's code.

Open the file `block_wikipedia.php` and look for the following line.

```
$form = '<form action="http://www.wikipedia.org/search-redirect.php"
id="searchform">';
```

Add a `target` attribute to the tag to direct searches to a new tab or browser window.

```
$form = '<form action="http://www.wikipedia.org/search-redirect.php"
id="searchform" target="_blank">';
```

## There's more...

Here are some pedagogical applications for the Wikipedia block:

- Asking students to compare Wikipedia entries in different languages as part of a language course
- Allowing students to find royalty free images for projects
- Allowing students to look up episode information for their favorite TV show

## See also

- Wikipedia easy links filter

# Adding links to Wikipedia

| Name | Wikipedia easy links |
|---|---|
| **Module type** | Filter |
| **Author** | Valery Fremaux |
| **Released** | 2006 |
| **Maintained** | No issues raised |
| **Languages** | Support for English, French, Spanish but should work in any language |
| **Compliance** | Good |
| **Documentation** | Online documentation and `readme.txt` file |
| **Errors** | None |

This is a very useful filter that allows teachers to mark words to form links that direct students to entries in Wikipedia.

## Getting ready

Download and install the directory named `wikipediacalls` into the `/moodle/filter/` directory. Enable the filter at **Site Administration** | **Modules** | **Filters** | **Manage filters**.

## How to do it...

The filter can be used to create links to Wikipedia entries around a course site, including text inside labels, web pages, forum posts, assignment descriptions, and so on.

When entering text in a Moodle editor, the Wikipedia filter code can be placed immediately after the target word in [square brackets]. Do not put spaces between the word and the brackets.

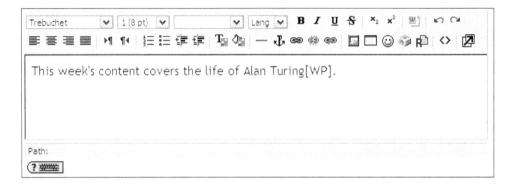

The most basic filter code is an upper case **[WP]** after the word you want linked. The word will then be passed as a search term to Wikipedia.

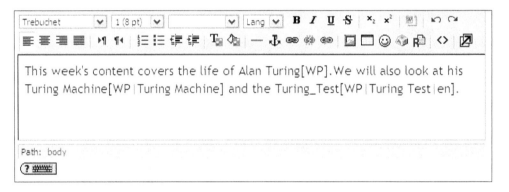

Two additional optional codes can be added to the WP code. If the desired search term differs from the word being linked, the desired search term(s) can be provided as a second code, separated from the WP code with a vertical bar **|**. This **|** symbol is accessible on a keyboard, usually by holding *Shift* and pressing the backslash \ key. Multiple search terms can be used in this second code, separated by spaces or underscore _ characters. The desired language for the target Wikipedia entry can be suggested as a third code, again following a vertical bar **|**. Language codes are two letter abbreviations, for example en, es, nl, ru, and so on.

If you would like to form the link around more than one word on a Moodle page, you can use an underscore character between words, for instance **Turing_Test[WP]**.

## How it works...

With the Wikipedia filter on, words followed by **[WP]** codes are rendered as links:

> This week's content covers the life of Alan Turing.We will also look at his Turing Machine and the Turing_Test.

Target words are turned into links to Wikipedia entries. Clicking on a link conveniently opens Wikipedia in a new tab or browser window.

## There's more...

Here are some ideas for how you could employ the Wikipedia filter in teaching:

 ▶  Directing students to specific Wikipedia entries related to current course topics

 ▶  The Wikipedia game: give students a starting point and challenge them to get to another article, distantly related, by clicking only links in Wikipedia entries. The winner can be the fastest or the student who uses the fewest links.

 ▶  Link to the Wikipedia main page, current news, featured articles or historical dates.

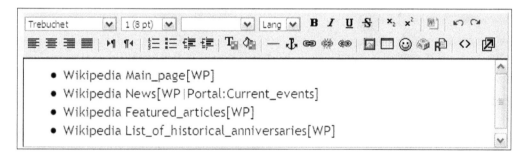

## See also

 ▶  Wikipedia block

# Searching for Tweets

| Name | Twitter Search |
|---|---|
| **Module Type** | Block |
| **Author** | Kevin Hughes |
| **Released** | 2010 |
| **Maintained** | Actively |
| **Languages** | Catalan, English, Hebrew |
| **Compliance** | Good |
| **Documentation** | None |
| **Errors** | None displayed |

Twitter is a popular system for micro-blogging. People can post short messages (or questions), and these messages can then be followed, searched, and viewed by anyone.

The Twitter Search block allows the results of a Twitter search to be displayed in a block.

## Getting ready

The Twitter Search block requires the cURL library to be enabled. Information about the cURL library and how to enable it is provided in the initial chapter of this book.

Unlike most modules, the block code for this module is downloadable from the block author's Moodle site. In order to download the block, you will need to log into that Moodle site; guest access is sufficient.

The module is also packaged as a `Tar` file and zipped using `gzip`; if you are using Windows or Mac, you may need an alternate compression program to unpack this module.

Unpack and copy the `twitter_search` directory into the `/moodle/blocks/` directory and visit the **Notifications** page.

## How to do it...

When added to a course, the block displays search results including the hash tag "#moodle". Click on the configuration icon to set up the block with your desired search.

On the configuration page, there are three settings.

## Configuring a Twitter Search block

Search Terms (Help): #mootau10
Number of tweets shown: 5
Time between automatic updates in ms (0 = never): 30000

Save changes

The search terms you use will define what results you get back. A useful link to a Twitter help file containing search tips is included next to this setting. Clicking this link opens the search help page in a new window. This page shows the variety of searches you can conduct, including potential to control alternatives, exclusions, and string searches. You can also specify the people involved in Tweets or their location, the times Tweets were sent, or the attitude of the person posting.

The second setting controls how many results you will receive and subsequently, how many Tweets are displayed in the block. Obviously the more Tweets shown, the greater the screen real-estate occupied by this block.

The block is capable of re-searching for new Tweets periodically. You can specify how often this happens using the third setting on the configuration page. The setting requires number of milliseconds, the default being 30000, which equates to 30 seconds. It would be inadvisable to use a lower figure, as this may overload your server if a large number of users are online and viewing the block. Setting this value to zero disables automatic refreshing of the search; users can still update the results manually.

## How it works...

The block shows a number of Tweets, up to the set limit.

At the bottom of the block there is an **update** link. Clicking this link will update the block without reloading the page, which is very convenient. Automatic updates happen in this fashion also, which is not distracting.

## There's more...

There are alternate means for displaying Tweets within a block. It is possible to access Tweets through an RSS feed. This alternative does not allow the same level of control over the search results that the Twitter Search block can achieve. Twitter also provides a view that can be squashed down to block size and embedded into an HTML block. This method is obviously more complicated than using a simple block, and would be beyond most teachers. This HTML block view also appears with animation, which could be distracting for students.

## Uses for Twitter searches in courses

Twitter is a social-networking system, but that does not mean it cannot be used within education contexts. Here are some pedagogical applications.

- ▸ Posting notices and opinions about an individual course, based on a specific hash tag for that course. Both teachers and students could contribute this way.

- ▸ Following the Tweets of a specific teacher or some other authoritarian figure related to the course.

- ▸ Following news about current topical events related to a course. Examples include political elections, sporting competitions, or natural disasters (or political sporting disasters).

- ▸ Providing links to information unrelated to the course that students may be interested in, and may be allowed to view as a reward.

Not all Moodle sites are used for educational purposes. Moodle is also a simple vehicle for hosting information and interactivity related to public events—conferences being a common example. In such circumstances, news and opinions about the event can be shown in a Twitter Search block, easily updated by anyone involved and allowing all to have a say.

## See also

- ▸ HTML block (standard in Moodle)

# 4
# Getting Around In Moodle

In this chapter, we will cover:

- ▶ Navigating within a course
- ▶ Navigating between courses
- ▶ Improving accessibility

## Introduction

A number of modules can assist users to navigate around a Moodle site.

### Navigating within a course

Moodle has a very simple navigation model. Links for a course are gathered on one page: the course main page. This means that resources and activities are usually only one link away. However, this shallow navigation model also has a downside—long course pages—which can lead to lots of annoying scrolling. Offering students a way to see the structure of a page, and directing them straight to parts of the page, can alleviate some of the finger strain needed for long pages. There are a number of blocks that attempt to simplify navigation within a course page:

- ▶ Course contents block
- ▶ YUI Menu
- ▶ Flyout Block Menu

## Navigating between courses

Moodle is used in institutions that have a small number of courses through to larger institutions with thousands of users and many courses. When a student is enrolled in more than one course, they may wish to navigate between the courses they are enrolled in easily. Administrators and teachers involved in more than one course may also wish to locate and oversee courses conveniently. There are a number of blocks that can be used to assist moving between courses in a Moodle site:

- My Courses 2 block
- Quick Course List block
- Related Courses block

## Improving accessibility

For many users, navigating around a Moodle page can be daunting, simply because they find it hard to read. There is one block that can assist visually impaired users:

- Accessibility block

# An easy table of contents

| Name | Course contents block |
|---|---|
| **Module type** | Block |
| **Author** | David Mudrák |
| **Released** | 2009 |
| **Maintained** | Actively |
| **Languages** | Czech, English |
| **Compliance** | Good |
| **Documentation** | Online documentation |
| **Errors** | None |

This is a very simple, but useful block that can automatically extrapolate and show a table of contents, based on the section titles in a course.

## Getting ready

Unzip and copy the Course contents block directory into the `/moodle/blocks/` directory and visit the **Notifications** page.

This block was created as a replacement for the Simple Navigation block, which is no longer maintained and doesn't seem to work on recent versions of Moodle.

## How to do it...

After the block is installed, it can be added to a course page by turning editing on and selecting **Course contents** from the **Blocks** menu.

There is no configuration for the block, which means it cannot be bent to your will, but also means that this block is extremely simple for anyone to use.

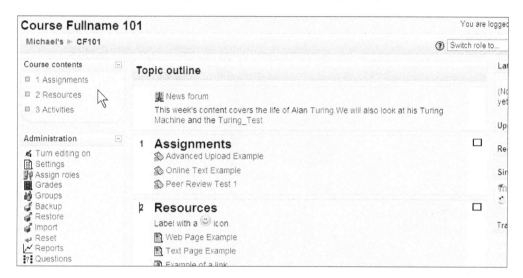

One aspect that I thought was slightly annoying was the addition of numbers to each topic title. This happened with both the weekly and topics formats. If you are game, you can remove these numbers with a simple change to the block code.

Open the block's main source code file called `block_course_contents.php` and locate the line that outputs the topic numbers. It should be around line 100 and contains the following code.

```
$text .= "<span class=\"section-number\">$i </span>";
```

This line can be commented out by adding two forward slashes at the beginning of the line like the following:

```
// $text .= "<span class=\"section-number\">$i </span>";
```

After saving this change, when the block is loaded, it will appear without the topic numbers.

Another aspect that cannot be changed, as there is no configuration, is title of the block. "Course contents" is relatively descriptive, but not the most appropriate title in English. To change the title, open the `/moodle/blocks/course_contents/lang/en_utf8/block_course_contents.php` file and set a new value for the `blockname` string. Alternately you can edit a local version of the language file through the facility at **Site Administration | Language | Language Editing**.

## See also

▶  YUI Menu

▶  Flyout Block Menu

# A menu block with the works

| Name | YUI Menu |
|------|----------|
| **Module type** | Block |
| **Author** | Alan Trick |
| **Released** | 2007 |
| **Maintained** | Very actively |
| **Languages** | English, French, Chinese (Traditional) |
| **Compliance** | Good |
| **Documentation** | Online documentation, `readme.txt` file |
| **Errors** | Issues with YUI Library |

The YUI Menu block allows students to navigate around the course main page and to access common activities and resources directly. This block duplicates the functionality of the **People** block, the **Activities** block, and the functionality of the **Administration** block as used by students. So with this block in place, those other blocks can be turned off and precious screen real-estate can be saved. Unfortunately the block does not replicate Administration functions for a teacher. If you do remove the Administration block, you will have to add it again when it comes time to alter course settings, conduct backups, restores, or imports, run reports, or access the files area.

## Getting ready

Unzip and copy the block directory into the `/moodle/blocks/` directory and visit the **Notifications** page.

## How to do it...

Add the block titled **Course Menu** from the **Blocks** menu. You may need to turn editing off before it performs correctly.

There seems to have been an ongoing battle for the block developer to keep up-to-date with changes in the Yahoo User Interface (YUI) library, which is used to achieve common JavaScript and Ajax functions in Moodle. If you do not see the tree menu, you may have a conflict between the version of the YUI library and the block. There are a number of fixes suggested on the Moodle **Modules and plugins** database page for the module.

When the block is added, you can configure what appears in the block and in what order the items appear. After turning editing on, click on the block's configuration icon and the following settings will appear.

## Configuring a Course Menu block

👁 Outline            ↓

👁 Calendar        ↑ ↓

👁 Gradebook    ↑ ↓

👁 Messages      ↑ ↓

👁 Forums          ↑ ↓

👁 Resources     ↑ ↓

👁 Assignments ↑ ↓

👁 Choices         ↑ ↓

👁 Quizzes         ↑ ↓

👁 Participants  ↑

Length of section intros:  `19`
Section intro truncation text: `...`
Section intro links action:  `Scroll screen to section ▾`

[ Save changes ]

Clicking the up and down arrows allows you to reorder topics. Clicking the eye icon for a topic allows it to be hidden or shown. These changes happen without reloading the page, but you will have to click the button labeled **Save changes** for these changes to take effect.

There are three settings at the bottom of the configuration page. The **Length of section intros** refers to the number of characters that are shown before a title is truncated. You might want to change this setting if your theme font has wider characters. When a title is truncated it is replaced with a three full-stop ellipsis "..." by default, but this can be changed by altering the second setting.

The third setting allows you to determine what happens when a link to a course topic or section is clicked. The default, labeled **Hide other sections** means that the page is reloaded, showing only the selected section with other sections hidden. The default behavior for a course is to show all topics, so it can be disconcerting for students when the page reloads showing only one section. To reverse this singular view, the user must click the icon to show all sections, which might not be intuitive for students.

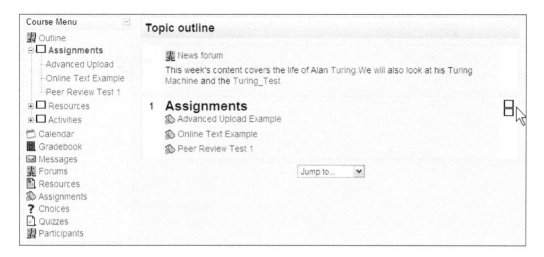

The second option for this setting **Scroll screen to section** changes this behavior. With this option selected, clicking a link scrolls the page so that the section is moved to the top of the page.

## See also

▸  Course contents block

▸  Flyout Block Menu

# A customizable menu block

| | |
|---|---|
| **Name** | Flyout Block Menu |
| **Module type** | Block |
| **Author** | Abrar Ullah, Jay Beavan |
| **Released** | 2009 |
| **Maintained** | Actively |
| **Languages** | English |
| **Compliance** | Abnormal configuration |
| **Documentation** | HTML instructions with block code |
| **Errors** | None |

The Flyout Block Menu allows users to create a hierarchical menu that appears dynamically as the user moves the mouse over links. The menu can include links to topics on the course page and links to URLs anywhere on the web.

## Getting ready

Unzip and copy the block directory into the `/moodle/blocks/` directory and visit the **Notifications** page. Be careful, the block zip file may contain an extra folder level at its root.

## How to do it...

**Turn editing on** and add the block from the **Blocks** menu. You will need to move the block to the left column as sub-menu links expand outwards to the right.

The block does not have a conventional configuration, so there is no configuration icon in the header of the block. Instead there is a link in the block body that takes you to a configuration page. This link only appears when editing is turned on.

On the non-standard configuration page there is a stepwise process to be followed in order to set up the menu. As changes are made in the form, the page updates and the menu is simulated at the bottom of the page. Initially the menu is empty.

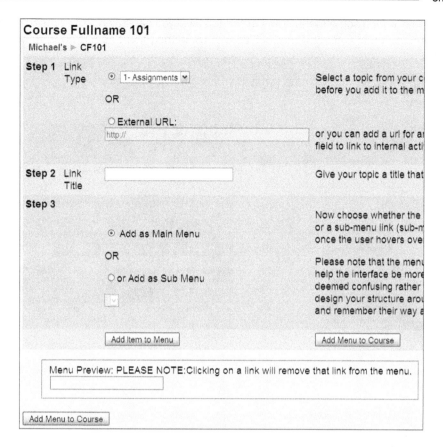

The first step is to choose whether you wish to include a link to a topic/week section in the course main page or a link to a URL on the web (or possibly somewhere on your site).

To create a link to a topic section, select the name of the topic from the drop-down list in the area of the configuration page identified as **Step 1**. The configuration does not attempt to extract the name of the topic, so you will still have to add a link title in **Step 2**. Skip over **Step 3** and click the button titled **Add Item to Menu**.

Adding a link to a URL can be achieved by checking the radio labeled **External URL** in **Step 1**. Add the full URL including the protocol (for example, `http://...`).

Once you have added some menu items at the top level you can begin to add menu items that will appear as sub-menu items. These will appear when the parent item is hovered over with the mouse.

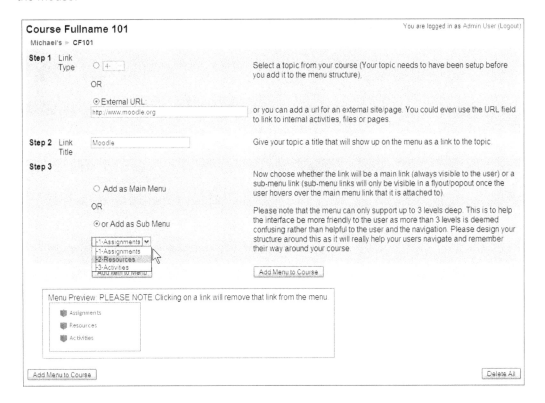

Menu items can be added as children to items at the top level or as children of sub-menu items. The block will show a hierarchy up to three levels deep.

Unfortunately, once a menu item is added it cannot be modified or moved. To modify an item, you need to delete the item and re-add it, with appropriate details, in the correct location. To remove a menu item, click on it in the simulated menu at the bottom of the configuration page.

When you have finished configuring the menu, click one of the two buttons labeled **Add Menu to Course** and the menu will appear in the block on the course page.

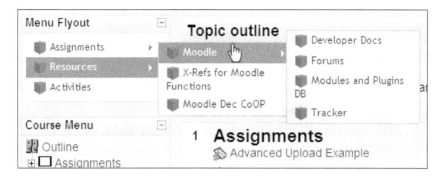

## How it works...

The hierarchy created on the configuration page is presented as a JavaScript menu in the block. It is a general design principle that Moodle should be able to function (at least for students) without JavaScript turned on. With this block, sub-menu items will not appear if JavaScript is turned off, which may affect the experience of some students.

When links to topics on the main page are clicked, the page refreshes with only that topic shown. This is not the default behavior of a course page, which usually shows all topics, so this may confuse users and possibly frustrate them if they cannot see how to show the other topics again. There is no configuration setting to change this behavior, as there is in other such blocks.

Links to URLs on the web appear in a new tab or browser window, so the current Moodle page is not lost. This is useful if the user is working on something on the current Moodle page.

The block is titled **Menu Flyout** on the page, which might not be intuitive to all users. There is no configuration setting to allow you to change this, so the only way to change the title to say "Course Links" is by changing the language file.

## There's more...

If you only want a table of contents to topics on a course page, then the Course contents block is probably a simpler choice. Where the Flyout Block Menu stands out is in its ability to link, to bring page topics and external links together in an organized fashion, in quite a compact form.

Here are some teaching applications for the block:

▶ Links directing students to optional readings on websites around the world, organized either by topics or some other structure

▶ Linking students to technical documentation organized using a conceptual hierarchy

See also

- ▸ Course contents block
- ▸ YUI Menu

# An organized My Courses block

| Name | My Courses 2 |
|---|---|
| **Module type** | Block |
| **Author** | Nate Baxley |
| **Released** | 2009 |
| **Maintained** | Somewhat |
| **Languages** | English |
| **Compliance** | Good |
| **Documentation** | `readme.txt` file |
| **Errors** | Error displayed under specific circumstances when error reporting is turned on |

The standard My Courses block shows the list of courses a user is involved in, so they can jump from one course to another without heading out to the site root page. The standard My Courses block is convenient, but it is not organized and can grow large with a long list of courses.

The My Courses 2 block is offered as a replacement for the standard My Courses block with courses organized hierarchically into categories.

## Getting ready

Unzip and copy the block directory into the `/moodle/blocks/` directory and visit the **Notifications** page.

## How to do it...

The My Courses 2 block draws from the global settings of standard My Courses block. You can set these at **Site Administration | Modules | Blocks | Courses**. For a very large site with many courses, administrators might wish to avoid seeing all courses in the My Courses block, unless they themselves are teaching in that course. The first global setting allows administrators to control what courses are shown to them in the My Courses block (standard and contributed).

Once the block is installed and added to a course page there are no settings that can be changed for the block. If this block is used, you might want to remove the standard My Courses block.

## How it works...

When the block is first seen by a user in a course, it shows the current category of the course. After that, the block 'remembers' its state on subsequent visits, keeping this information in the Moodle database.

## See also

▸ Quick Course List block
▸ Related Courses block

# Finding a course by name

| | |
|---|---|
| **Name** | Quick Course List |
| **Module type** | Block |
| **Author** | Mike Worth |
| **Released** | 2009 |
| **Maintained** | Yes (there's not much to it) |
| **Languages** | English |
| **Compliance** | Good |
| **Documentation** | None |
| **Errors** | None |

If you have a site with many courses, then searching for a course can sometimes be a challenge. The Quick Course List block offers a solution. As a user types into the search box, it tries to match the search string with substrings of the course titles and course short titles of all courses on a site.

## Getting ready

Unzip and copy the block directory into the `/moodle/blocks/` directory and visit the **Notifications** page.

## How to do it...

This block is designed to work only on the site root page.

The block will list all matching courses on the site, even if the user is not involved in the course. Because of this, access to the block is limited. Only users with a role that includes permission to see the block will see it; by default this includes administrators, course creators and teachers. You can change the permissions of users with specific roles at **Site Administration | Users | Permissions | Define roles**. For example, if you wanted to prevent teachers from seeing the block, you can click the configuration icon to edit the role permissions for teachers.

Change the **Use Quickcourse List** permission to **Not set** and click the button labeled **Save changes** at the bottom of the page.

Once you are happy with the list of users that can access the block, you can add the block on the site root page. Go to the site root page and **Turn editing on**. You can then select the block from the **Blocks** menu there.

## How it works...

When you start typing into the textbox in the block a list of courses appears. The list is a filtered subset of all courses. The filtering is done by attempting to find the query string as a substring inside either the course name or short name of each course.

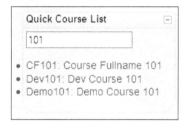

## See also

▶ My Courses 2 block

▶ Related Courses block

# Getting between Related Courses

| Name | Related Courses block |
| --- | --- |
| **Module type** | Block |
| **Author** | Marty Jacobs |
| **Released** | 2008 |
| **Maintained** | Actively |
| **Languages** | English |
| **Compliance** | Good |
| **Documentation** | Online documentation |
| **Errors** | None |

Meta courses allow you to bring participants in multiple courses together. For instance, if an institution has an area of teaching with multiple courses taught inside it, it may be useful to bring the participants of courses in that teaching area together into another 'meta' course, which allows them to communicate and interact together in matters that involve everyone in that area. The same could apply to year levels or discipline groupings. Another application of meta courses is for classes that occur over more than one teaching period, with each period having a separate Moodle course.

A meta course can bring together multiple 'child' courses and a course can be a child of multiple 'meta' courses.

If you are viewing the course page of a meta course or a child course, you may want to move from that course to the related course. The Related Courses block shows a list of related courses and allows quick navigation between them.

## Getting ready

The block code is not distributed in the newer all-in-one-folder fashion. Within the `zip` file, locate the `blocks` folder. Inside this is a folder titled `related_courses`; copy this folder including the file inside to your `moodle/blocks/` directory. Also inside the `zip` file is a `lang` folder. Copy this folder, including the nested folder and file, to the new `moodle/blocks/related_courses/` directory. With the files in place, visit the **Notifications** page and the block should install.

## How to do it...

If you do not have any meta courses and you want to test this block, you can create a meta course quite easily. Go to **Site Administration | Courses | Add/edit courses** and click on the button labeled **Add a new course**. Create the new course in the same way you would create any other course, except for the final setting in the **General** settings area, which is labeled **Is this a meta course?**. Select **Yes** for this option.

When the course is created, you can add select courses that will become child courses of your new meta course. Select more than one while holding the *Ctrl* key and clicking.

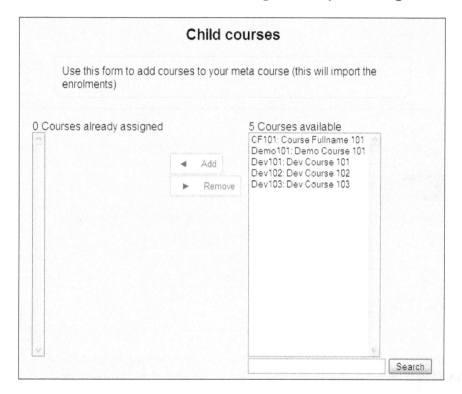

Once a meta course is created, courses can be added and removed as children by clicking the **Child courses** link from the **Administration** menu in the meta course.

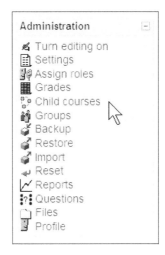

The Related Courses block can then be added to the meta course and the child courses.

## How it works...

In meta courses, the list of child courses is queried and displayed in the block.

In child courses, the list of parent meta courses is queried and displayed. Only one course will appear if the course is a child of only one meta course (that would probably be the norm).

## See also

▸ My Courses 2 block

▸ Quick Course List block

# Improving accessibility

| Name | Accessibility |
|---|---|
| **Module Type** | Block |
| **Author** | Mark Johnson |
| **Released** | 2009 |
| **Maintained** | Very actively |
| **Languages** | English, German, Spanish |
| **Compliance** | Good |
| **Documentation** | Little (but little needed) |
| **Errors** | None |

Allowing users to choose higher contrast color schemes and larger font sizes can assist visually impaired users to overcome reading difficulties. The Accessibility block allows users to change the way pages are displayed to them in Moodle.

 The Accessibility block may alter the appearance of your site theme. It may also affect the behavior and usability of modules in your site that rely on color to express meaning.

## Getting ready

Unzip and copy the block directory into the /moodle/blocks/ directory and visit the **Notifications** page.

## How to do it...

As well as installing the block code, you will need to make a change to the theme used on your site. If more than one theme is used, all themes will need to be modified. The change is not significant.

Navigate to the /moodle/themes/ directory and you will see a folder for each available theme. Find the theme you are using and navigate inside that folder. You will find a number of files and one will be named header.html. Open this file in a text editor.

Inside the file add a new line just before the `</head>` tag. Copy the following lines to the file at that location:

```
<link title="access_stylesheet" rel="stylesheet" href="<?php if($CFG-
>wwwroot != $CFG->httpswwwroot) {echo $CFG->httpswwwroot;} else {echo
$CFG->wwwroot;} ?>/blocks/accessibility/userstyles.php" type="text/
css" />
```

 If you alter a theme and later update the theme, changes you have made will be overwritten, and will need to be made again.

Once the block is installed, and the theme header file had been updated, you will be able to add the **Accessibility** block from the **Blocks** menu.

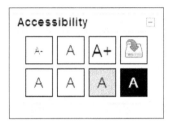

## How it works...

The block uses iconic symbols as buttons that can control the font size and contrast on the current page. Moving the mouse over each icon gives a textual description. When a button is clicked, it takes a few seconds for the desired change to come about.

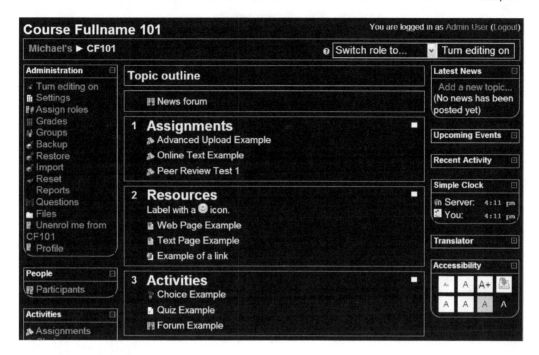

Changes remain until the browser is closed. Clicking on the **Save Setting** icon (top-right in the block) causes the current settings to be saved to the database between logins. For both font size and contrast levels there is an icon that resets the view to theme default settings.

## There's more...

Some teachers may be aware of students who have visual impairments and may benefit from such a block. In some areas, legislative requirements may force certain accessibility standards to be enforced.

Besides providing an aid to people with visual impairments, this block might also be useful to students learning *about* visual impairments, or perhaps learning about the legislation relating to disabilities, or possibly even learning about how to create websites that assist the visually impaired.

# 5
# Effective Use of Space

In this chapter, we will cover:

- ▸ Squeezing main content into a block
- ▸ Collapsing content
- ▸ Using tabs in course pages
- ▸ Using monthly sections for longer courses
- ▸ Combining online users and people

## Introduction

Moodle employs a very simple navigation model. Course links are all shown on the course main page, so users are only one click away from a resource or activity. However, this simple, shallow navigation comes at a cost—long course pages.

In a real course with content that spans an entire teaching period, the length of course pages can grow many screens. Apart from the annoying scrolling needed to locate links, the sheer number of links can cause relevant content to become lost in a tangle of sameness. These modules allow teachers to focus student attention to what is current and important.

This chapter looks at modules that can be added to Moodle that attempt to address the need to better manage the space in a course page and offer easier navigation to users.

## Adding main page content into a block

One way to remove content from the central sections of a course main page is to put it into a block. It is possible to put links to resources and activities in a block. As well as creating space in the central area, this creates the potential to highlight important links.

- Side Bar Block

## Collapsing content

One easy way to use space more effectively is to collapse content down and allow users to expand what they need when they need it. A number of well designed course formats can provide this potential. Collapsing can happen around hierarchically related resources and activities to form a tree-like structure, or around whole topics or weeks:

- Topicstree course format
- Collapsed Topics format
- Collapsed Weeks format

## Using tabs in course pages

Tabs are another way of taking a regular course page and dividing its content into smaller chunks. There are a number of formats that attempt this:

- Topics Tabs format
- Weekly Tabs format
- OneTopic format

## Using monthly sections for longer courses

If time is an important factor in a course, but the course runs over many weeks, then changing the time scale to months can reduce the number of sections needed, and also the space used.

- Months course format

## Combining online users and people

The **People** block contains only a single link to the **Participants** list. Another related block is the **Online Users** block. Combining these two can help reduce the space used for blocks, while still allowing access to these practical facilities.

▸   Lonely People Block (patch)

# Squeezing main page content into a block

| Name | Side Bar Block |
|---|---|
| **Module type** | Block |
| **Author** | Justin Filip, Mike Churchward, Fernando Oliveira |
| **Released** | 2006 |
| **Maintained** | Actively |
| **Languages** | English |
| **Compliance** | Good |
| **Documentation** | Online documentation, readme.txt file |
| **Errors** | None |

This block can contain content that you would normally add in the sections of a course main page. The block displays links to activities and resources, just as they would normally appear on the course main page.

 Don't be discouraged by the mention of incompatibility on the module's entry in the Moodle **Modules and plugins** database. This block has been around for some time and has been updated for several versions. It works well with Moodle 1.9.x.

## Getting ready

Unzip and copy the Side Bar block directory into the /moodle/blocks/ directory then visit the **Notifications** page.

## How to do it...

There is a global block setting associated with this block. After installing the block you might want to check it at **Site Administration | Modules | Blocks | Side Bar**.

At first it may not be clear what this setting controls. The block contains a pseudo course section and it keeps information about section links in the same database table as other sections in a course. A normal course will have between three to twelve normal topic/week sections and a teacher is free to add or remove sections. So as not to interfere with these normal sections, the Side Bar Block's pseudo sections begin their numbering at 1000. You would only need to change this setting if you have a single course which has 1000 or more normal sections, which seems very unlikely (and inadvisable). It doesn't matter how many courses you have and how many sections there are in total, only the maximum number of sections in any single course main page matters.

On your course page, **Turn editing on** and you can add the block, like any other block, from the **Blocks** menu. It is listed as **Side Bar**.

With editing still turned on, click on the configuration icon for the block. The block itself has only one setting, but it is an appropriate one. Because the block can be applied to a variety of uses, the block title can be configured. Consider the application for the block and set a title that reflects this, such as "Homework" or "Reference Materials".

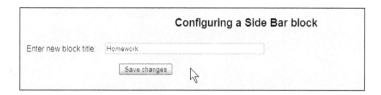

You can have more than one instance of this block in a course, so if you have multiple applications in mind, you may consider separating them over multiple block instances.

In the block, you will see the same menus for activities and resources that you would see in any normal course section. Selecting an item from these menus allows you to create and configure a new activity or resource in the normal way.

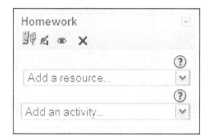

When you have added activities and resources, the links to these appear in the block as they would in a section of the central column of the main page. Consideration is needed for the length of titles shown in the block. Titles and labels will wrap, but there is clearly less width in the block, compared to a normal section.

Links in the block can be moved, updated (configured), deleted or hidden, but the block does not allow Ajax dynamic editing; in other words, each change requires a page reload.

One nice feature is the ability to move activities and resources from the block to the page and in the other direction also. In the block, when you click on the up-down icon (labeled as **Move** when you hover the mouse over it), you can move the relevant link to any point on the block or to a section in the course main page.

You can also achieve the opposite—you can shift links from a section in the course main page to the **Side Bar** block. If you have Ajax dynamic editing turned on, you won't be able to drag links onto the block as you can between course sections. To achieve a move from course section to the block, you can turn Ajax editing off; this can be done in your personal profile (it is an advanced setting labeled 'Ajax and JavaScript'). There is, however, a quicker way to do this without turning Ajax editing off. When a page loads, it will first load without the Ajax editing controls, and then an overlay will be superimposed over the page. There is usually a short delay before this overlay appears while the entire page is finalized. During this delay, you can click on the up-down icon for an activity or resource in the main page, and doing so will take you to a page where you can reposition the link to a new location, including locations on the **Side Bar** block.

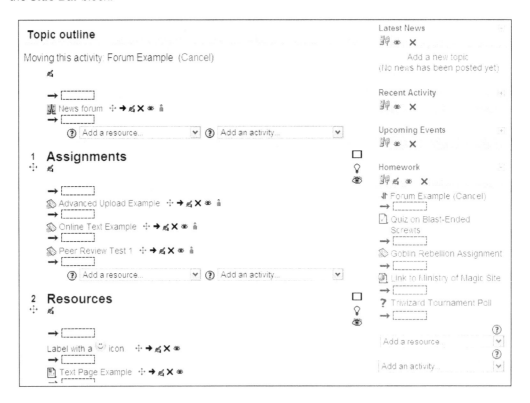

## How it works...

With editing turned off, links appear in the **Side Bar** block as they normally do on the course main page.

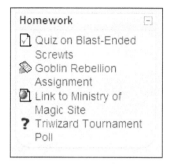

When **Side Bar** block links to activities and resources are clicked, the activities and resources appear on a page by themselves as normal.

## There's more...

The Side Bar Block allows you to add the same links you could add elsewhere on your course main page, so how is it useful? Well, it's not the course overview and it's not a topic or week section. It is instead a place where you can add content that is, perhaps, related to the course in a sideways manner. Here are some examples:

- ▸ Links to current topical issues or news
- ▸ Activities half-way related to your course, but more fun than fact
- ▸ Links to the latest movies, games, or TV shows, that students will enjoy viewing as a reward when they have finished their work
- ▸ Reference materials used throughout a course
- ▸ A grouping of links that will be important to students throughout the semester, for example, assessment items

## See also

- ▸ HTML block (standard in Moodle)
- ▸ Flyout Block Menu

# Organizing tree-based content

| | |
|---|---|
| **Name** | Topicstree course format |
| **Module type** | Course format |
| **Author** | Eloy Lafuente (stronk7) |
| **Released** | 2008 |
| **Maintained** | Limited |
| **Languages** | English, Spanish (but should work in any language) |
| **Compliance** | Good |
| **Documentation** | Online documentation, `readme.txt` |
| **Errors** | None |

This course format allows you to compact topics down by utilizing the structure of nested items.

## Getting ready

Unzip the module's source directory to `/moodle/course/format/`. Once copied, you can use the format straight away.

## How to do it...

Once added, the format can be chosen from the **Settings** page. Click **Settings** in the course's **Administration** block. You will find the **Topics Tree format** listed as one of the course formats.

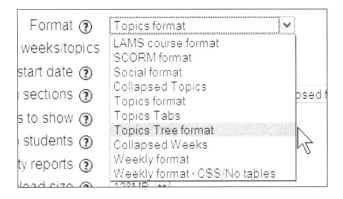

After selecting the **Topics Tree format**, save the course settings. You will not see any change if you have editing turned on. Turn editing off to see the effect of the format.

Activities and resources under each topic should be listed as a tree. If all the items in the topic are at the same level they will all appear. Nested items will not appear at first.

The tree structure of each topic is based on the hierarchical nesting of items in the topic. **Turn editing on** and look for the right-facing arrow next to each item.

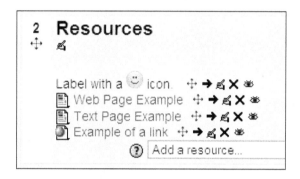

Clicking an arrow will demote an item, causing it to become a child of items above it. You can demote and promote items to build the tree hierarchy.

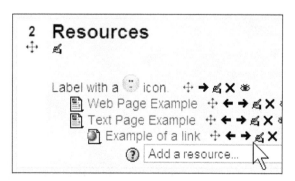

Once you are satisfied with the hierarchy you have created, **Turn editing off** to see the effect. Items that are not demoted (not indented) will appear. If items have children then a ± symbol will be displayed next to them.

Sub-items appear after clicking on the ± next to their parent. The tree structure unfolds and folds up again as the user expands and contracts the tree.

## There's more...

This format is useful for compacting the content of a topic. It also encourages the creation of a hierarchy of importance in the items of a topic. Most users should be familiar with tree metaphor used by this format, however, the need to click the ± symbol to expand the tree is not entirely obvious. It is possible that students may incorrectly click the activity or resource link in an attempt to expand that part of the tree.

## See also

▶ Collapsed Weeks format
▶ Collapsed Topics format

# Collapsing sections

| Name | Collapsed Topics course format, |
| --- | --- |
| | Collapsed Weeks course format |
| Module type | Course format |
| Author | Gareth Barnard |
| Released | 2009 |

| Maintained | Very Actively |
|---|---|
| **Languages** | English (but should work in any language) |
| **Compliance** | Good |
| **Documentation** | Online documentation, `readme.txt` |
| **Errors** | None |

These two formats allow topics or weeks to be collapsed to minimize space used. The topic/week sections can then be expanded dynamically.

## Getting ready

Unzip both directories to the `/moodle/course/format/` directory. You do not need to visit the **Notifications** page for course formats. You can use them right away.

## How to do it...

Go to the **Settings** page for a course. Select either of the formats from the **Format** menu. The **Collapsed Topics format** appears with all topics initially collapsed.

The **Collapsed Weeks format** shows the current calendar week at first.

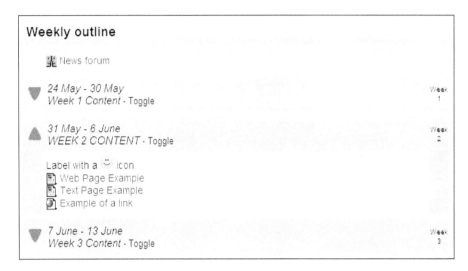

With either format, the bar at the top of each topic/week can be clicked to open and close that section. The state of expanded and hidden topics is retained during the user's browser session, but returns to the initial state when the user returns to the site later.

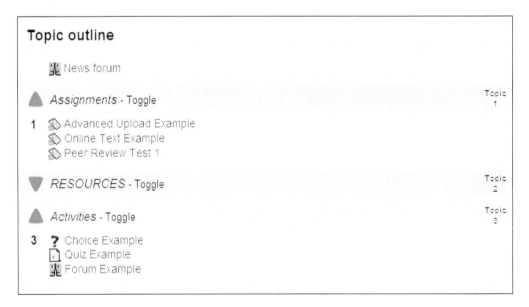

The text titles of weeks and topics are subsumed by the toggle bar at top of each section, so these are not unnecessarily repeated. This is another good use of space.

## There's more...

The nature of the Collapsed Topics and Collapsed Weeks formats allows a long course page to be condensed, and a single week or topic to be focused upon. It is much more convenient than the built-in functionality used to view a single week or topic in isolation. It is more intuitive to use than the Topicstree course format, however it does not offer the ability to create a hierarchical organization.

## See also

▶   Topicstree course format

# Creating dynamic tabs

| Name | Topics Tabs |
|---|---|
|  | Weekly Tabs |
| **Module type** | Course format |
| **Author** | Amr Hourani |
| **Released** | 2008 |
| **Maintained** | Actively |
| **Languages** | English (but should work in any language) |
| **Compliance** | Uses JQuery JavaScript/Ajax library instead of standard YUI library |
| **Documentation** | None |
| **Errors** | Not all necessary strings translated |

Using these course formats, course page topics or weeks can be displayed under tabs. Clicking on a tab causes the page to scroll to the desired section.

## Getting ready

Uncompress both the `topicstabs` and `weekstabs` directories to the `/moodle/course/format/` directory. You do not need to visit the **Notifications** page to install these course formats.

The `topicstabs` format is distributed in a `rar` file, so you may need a standalone compression program to extract this new format directory.

## How to do it...

Click on the **Settings** link from the course **Administration** menu and choose the **Topics Tabs format**, then save the settings.

The **Topics Tabs format** takes each topic, including the course overview section and turns these into tabs. It also collects together the blocks that would normally appear around the outside of the page and puts these into a tab as well.

The **Weekly Tabs format** has a similar look to the **Topics Tabs format**, with weeks appearing by number. Arrows are also shown on either side of the centered tab section; these arrows allow the user to navigate forwards and backwards.

Activities and resources can be added to sections as normal, and the links to these activities and resources work as normal. Ajax page features are disabled when these formats are used, which means there is no ability to drag (move), promote/demote, delete or hide/show activities and resources without reloading the page. Blocks can be manipulated using the Ajax functionality on the **Blocks** tab.

With either theme, there was a noticeably longer page load time. The block does not use the normal YUI JavaScript library, instead of using the non-standard JQuery library, which might be causing some delay. Re-building the page as tabs also seems to cause delay.

Being a course format, this module is not configurable without modifying the format code. This is rather annoying as there are a number of aspects that most users would want to change. For example, the colors used for tabs are not horrible, but it would not blend in with most themes. It would be nice to control which tab opens as the default tab.

The names of the tabs are fixed. These two formats do not attempt to extract the names of sections from the section titles (as is done in other formats). The author claims this is due to a lack of space on tabs.

Neither format attempts to keep track of the tab the user was last viewing. Whenever the course page is reloaded, users are taken to the **Blocks** tab.

Despite these deficiencies, the format does a competent job of reducing the space consumed by sections and presenting those sections dynamically, even with a flourish of animation. If you are attempting to create course pages with a bit more dazzle, either of these formats may suit your needs.

## See also

▸ OneTopic course format

# Simplifying single section display with tabs

| | |
|---|---|
| **Name** | OneTopic (a.k.a. Un tema a la vez) |
| **Module type** | Course format |
| **Author** | David Herney Bernal García |
| **Released** | 2009 |
| **Maintained** | Actively |
| **Languages** | English, Spanish (but should work in any language) |
| **Compliance** | Good |
| **Documentation** | Online documentation (Spanish only) |
| **Errors** | None |

This format takes the method of displaying a single topic at a time, used in the standard Topics format, and simplifies this with tabs at the top of each section

## Getting ready

Unzip the module's source directory to `/moodle/course/format/`. You can then use the format straight away.

## How to do it...

Visit the **Settings** page for your course and scroll down in the **General** settings area to the **Format** setting. Choose the **Topics in tabs** format (not to be confused with the **Topics Tabs** format described earlier), then save the settings.

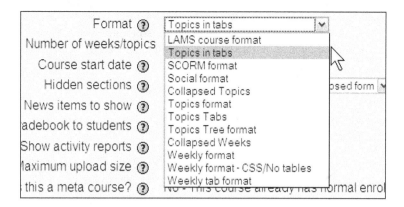

The OneTopic format, or as it is written in Spanish, the "Un tema a la vez" format, applies a keep-it-simple philosophy to minimizing use of page space, while adding a level of usability not present in the standard **Topics format**. With the standard **Topics format** it is possible to select and focus on one topic or week, then move to other sections by selecting them from the **Jump to...** drop-down menu.

When selected, the OneTopic format forces the course page to be shown one section at a time. To navigate to other sections, the user can click on the appropriate tab at the top of the page. This is more convenient and obvious than the **Jump to...** menu (which is still made available).

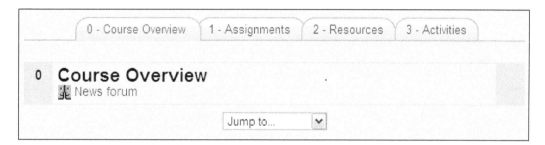

The tabs are named according to the titles of each section on the course page.

## How it works...

When a tab is selected, the whole page reloads. This is not as convenient as jumping to the section without having to reload the page, but it works solidly.

The format uses the tabs that are part of the Moodle HTML library, so these will blend in nicely with any theme that you may be using. The tabs will also function as the user expects.

Because the OneTopic format does not attempt to use any fancy dynamic overlay to present the course page, normal Ajax functionality still works as expected, which means you can move, promote, demote, hide, and delete without reloading the page.

## There's more...

One aspect that you might wish to change is the numbering on **Topic** tabs. Because this format is simple, the coding is also easy to change.

Open the file `/moodle/course/format/onetopic/format.php` and scroll down to line 126 and you should find the following:

```
'<font style="white-space:nowrap">' . s($section.$strsummary) . "</
font>", s($section.$strsummary));
```

Change this line by removing the `$section` variable and the full stop used to concatenate this string to the next. You should end up with the following version of the line:

```
'<font style="white-space:nowrap">' . s($strsummary) . "</font>",
s($strsummary));
```

Scroll up to around line 116 and you will see where the `$strsummary` variable is set. To remove the dashes from the strings, delete that `' - '` and the following concatenation (full stop) operator. Be sure to do this for both the `if` and `else` blocks. You should end up with the following lines of code:

```
if (strlen($strsummary) < 57) {
    $strsummary = $strsummary;
} else {
    $strsummary = substr($strsummary, 0, 60).'...';
}
```

After saving these changes, the tabs should appear unnumbered at the top of the course page.

If you alter a course format and later update that format with a new version from the author, changes you have made will be overwritten, and will need to be made again.

## See also

▸ Topics Tabs format

▸ Weekly Tabs format

# Using monthly sections for longer courses

| | |
|---|---|
| **Name** | Months course format |
| **Module type** | Course format |
| **Author** | Amr Hourani and Anthony Borrow |
| **Released** | 2008 |
| **Maintained** | Limited |
| **Languages** | English, French, Spanish |
| **Compliance** | Good |
| **Documentation** | Online documentation |
| **Errors** | None |

If you are running a course that stretches over 12 weeks or more, you may start to see your course page growing very large when the weekly format is used. The Months course format allows you to change the time scale of a course from weeks to months.

## Getting ready

Unzip the source directory to `/moodle/course/format/`. You can then use the format straight away.

## How to do it...

Visit the course settings page by clicking the link labeled **Settings** on the **Administration** block. Select the **Monthly format** from the **Format** list. Save changes to the settings.

## How it works...

The format recognizes the time-span of the course and establishes a section for each month involved, even if your course only partially covers a month. This could be somewhat annoying if your course begins near the very end of a month.

The effect of moving from the weekly format to this monthly format is a huge saving in space. You can still have the benefits of a time-based format, but with fewer sections in a longer course.

## See also...

> ▶  Flexible web page course format (see **Modules and plugins** database)

# Combining online users and people

| Name | Lonely People Block |
|---|---|
| **Module type** | Patch |
| **Author** | Nicole Hansen, et al. |
| **Released** | 2006 |
| **Maintained** | Limited |
| **Languages** | Not applicable |
| **Compliance** | Patch file |

| Documentation | None |
|---|---|
| Errors | None |

The **People** block contains a single link to the **Participants** list. The **Online Users** block shows people who have visited the course page recently. What if there was a way to combine these two related blocks? Well, there is, and it is another simple way to claim back more valuable screen real estate.

## Getting ready

The **Lonely People Block** is not really a block (and it's not a dating service either), it involves a patch. In other words, you are replacing part of the standard Moodle code. This might sound dangerous, but it's really quite a simple change.

## How to do it...

There are two ways to achieve this patch. The first is to copy the provided patch file over the existing **Online Users** block code.

On the Moodle **Modules and plugins** entry for this patch, instead of left-clicking to download the module code, right-click on the download link and save the file named `block_online_users.php` to your computer. This file will be copied to the `/moodle/blocks/online_users/` directory, but before you copy the file, be sure to back up the `block_online_users.php` file that is already there (just in case).

The problem with overwriting the standard block code is that the patch file may not be up-to-date with changes in the standard **Online Users** block. Instead of overwriting the block code, you can make the following addition to the existing `block_online_users.php` file, just before the return statement at the bottom of the file. This is the only part of the patch that is needed. This addition has also been updated to abide by the current role identification method.

```
if(
    $COURSE->id!=SITEID &&
    has_capability('moodle/course:viewparticipants', $context)
) {
    $this->content->text .=
        '<div style="text-align:center;font-size:small">'.
        '<a title="'.get_string('listofallpeople').'" href="'.
        $CFG->wwwroot.'/user/index.php?id='.
        $this->instance->pageid.'">'.
        '<img src="'.$CFG->pixpath.
        '/i/users.gif" height="16" width="16" alt="'.
        get_string('listofallpeople').
```

```
                    '" style="vertical-align:text-top" /> '.
                  get_string('participants').'</a></div>';
     }
```

With the block code changed, there are no configuration changes that need to be made. The **Online Users** block will appear as normal, with a link to the **Participants** list at the bottom. The only change you might like to make is to remove the **People** block, which is now redundant.

This patch is a simple change, but with screen real estate, sometimes every bit counts.

## See also

▶   YUI Menu block

# 6
# Assessing Students

In this chapter, we will cover:

- ► Assignment alternatives
- ► Involving students in assessment design
- ► Extending quizzes
- ► Simple formative feedback
- ► Encouraging competition

## Introduction

Assessment is a key part of education. For many students, the opportunity to earn marks through assessment is a driving motivator. Electronic assessment allows teachers to conduct a wider variety of assessment, and to do so more efficiently than traditional forms of assessment.

In this chapter, we will look at assessment-related Moodle modules, large and small, and some that are capable of involving students in innovative ways.

## Assignment alternatives

An assignment is a significant form of assessment, allowing students to demonstrate the understanding they have developed over a period of learning.

Many teachers struggle to break away from traditional essays and reports. As well as the assignment types available in core Moodle, there are some well constructed, contributed assignment types that are sure to lure the most ardent traditionalist away from "red pen on paper".

- ▶ Peer Review Assignment Type
- ▶ NanoGong Assignment Type
- ▶ UploadPDF Assignment Type

## Involving students in assessment design

Who said writing questions was the teacher's job? For students, the challenge of creating questions encourages them to think in a new and different way about the material they are studying. The incentive of being able to create questions that may be used in their own future assessment is also a thrill.

- ▶ Question Creation module

## Extending quizzes

Like many parts of Moodle, the Quiz module is extensible. New question types can be added to the Quiz module so that teachers can produce more creative questions and challenge learners from a wider range.

- ▶ Drag-and-drop matching question type
- ▶ Drag-and-drop ordering question type
- ▶ Image target question type

## Simple formative feedback

Students are motivated to earn marks, but that doesn't mean you can't sneak in a bit of formative assessment without them realizing it. Simply encouraging students to anticipate small snippets of the material can probe their knowledge, reinforcing their correct understandings and challenging their misunderstandings.

- ▶ Hidden Text filter

## Encouraging competition

It is a disservice to delude students into believing that they standout when they are in fact falling behind. Displaying the highest standard for assignments and other assessable items on a leader-board can motivate students to compete, while recognizing those who are excelling.

► Course Results block

# Using peer assessment

| Name | Peer Review |
| --- | --- |
| Module type | Assignment type |
| Author | Michael de Raadt |
| Released | 2010 |
| Maintained | Actively |
| Languages | English |
| Compliance | Good |
| Documentation | Online documentation, help files |
| Errors | None displayed |

Peer assessment can benefit students by causing them to evaluate the work of their peers. Evaluation is a higher order thinking skill, and requiring students to evaluate the work of others can enhance their learning experience. Other benefits are student involvement in the assessment process and the fact that they will receive more than just instructor feedback.

When used in conjunction with communication tools, peer assessment has the potential to encourage a learning community. This is particularly useful when students are studying in the Moodle environment, but physically separated from each other.

The Workshop module—a core Moodle module, was the first contributed Moodle module. It brought peer assessment to Moodle, exemplifying the constructivist nature that has driven Moodle development over the years. However, in recent years, the Workshop module has not been maintained, and is disabled by default in Moodle. The Workshop module is currently being revived for Moodle 2.0 and shows great promise.

Various peer assessment tools (outside Moodle) can reduce the quantity of marking for teachers, by relying on the student feedback as a basis for marking. This can be somewhat controversial when student feedback is the only source of grades. The Peer Review Assignment Type uses peer-feedback moderated by teachers as the basis for marks.

The Peer Review Assignment Type attempts to simplify the peer assessment experience of the Workshop module for both teachers and students. Only one deadline is needed (students can even submit late and still be involved); most students will submit then immediately move on to reviewing, while the assignment is fresh in their minds. The Peer Review Assignment Type manages the relationships between students automatically, so all the teacher has to do is set up the assignment, then moderate reviews after the assignment deadline.

## Getting ready

Being an Assignment Type, you need to unzip the `peerreview` directory into the `/moodle/mod/assignment/type/` directory before visiting the **Notifications** page.

## How to do it...

Once installed, a Peer Review assignment can be added from the **Add an activity...** menu. You will find it nested below **Assignments**.

As it is an Assignment Type, the Peer Review Assignment Type has the same **General** settings as other Assignment Types (including a name, description, grade value, and due date). There are four settings specific to this Assignment Type listed in the **Peer Review** section of the configuration page.

The first setting allows the teacher to decide if submissions will be in the form of a submitted file or text entered online in a WYSIWYG editor. If **Submitted document** is selected, the maximum file size and file type must be specified. These two settings should be made while keeping in mind that students will be downloading and reviewing each other's documents. Keep the maximum file size as low as practically possible, otherwise file transfer problems may arise. A file type that all students can work with should be selected. So, for instance, if students have a mix of Office 2003, Office 2007, and OpenOffice, using the `.doc` file type would allow all students be able to open and review submitted documents.

Each student is expected to complete two reviews and this is seen as part of the learning experience. The final setting in this section allows a reward value to be set for each of the reviews the student completes.

With the assignment configuration complete, click on **Save and Display** and you will be taken to a page where review criteria can be written.

On this page, the criteria descriptions and values can be set. Some help is provided on writing good criteria; this is worth reading.

For each criterion, you can enter a textual description that will appear to the student with the assignment description. This can include HTML tags if formatting is needed. For each criterion, a second alternate description can be provided, which can contain information that you want hidden from students before they submit (such as answers or test data); this is only shown to students as they complete reviews. A value also needs to be set for each criterion.

The values of criteria and the reward students will receive for completing reviews need to add up to the total grade value for the assignment. At the bottom of the **Criteria** page, there is a JavaScript driven calculator that indicates if values sum correctly.

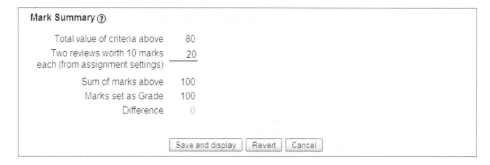

Once you have entered the criteria, save them and you will be taken to the description of the assignment showing the criteria added at the end. Students will also see a facility to submit a file, or a WYSIWYG editor if online-text is to be entered.

With the **Description** and the **Criteria** set, there is nothing to do until students have submitted and the assignment deadline has passed.

If you are running this Assignment Type on a test server and want to see how it works, you will need to set up at least five dummy student accounts and use these to submit assignments and complete reviews.

After students have submitted and completed reviews, they are shown a wealth of information about their submission, reviews they have conducted, and reviews they have received from their peers and teachers. Students have the opportunity to flag reviews they are unhappy with.

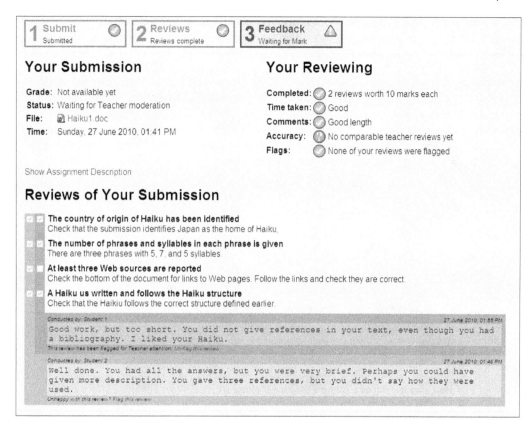

When students have submitted and reviewed, it is the teacher's job to resolve conflicts. The Peer Review Assignment Type shows a submission table, like other Assignment Types, but adds information about review relationships and conflicts.

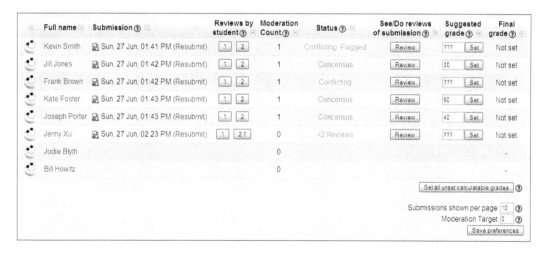

The teacher must add additional "moderation" reviews to override reviews that are conflicting. The tail end of the submissions list must also be reviewed by the teacher if there are not sufficient reviews for the system to suggest a mark.

When conducting moderation reviews, the teacher is provided with information that students do not get to see. The teacher can see which criteria students have checked, and also the comments they have written about the submission currently being moderated. Teachers can see which student conducted each review and how long they spent reviewing. The teacher has access to a textbox, in which they can add and save comments to be re-used later. Multiple markers have access to this same saved comments list.

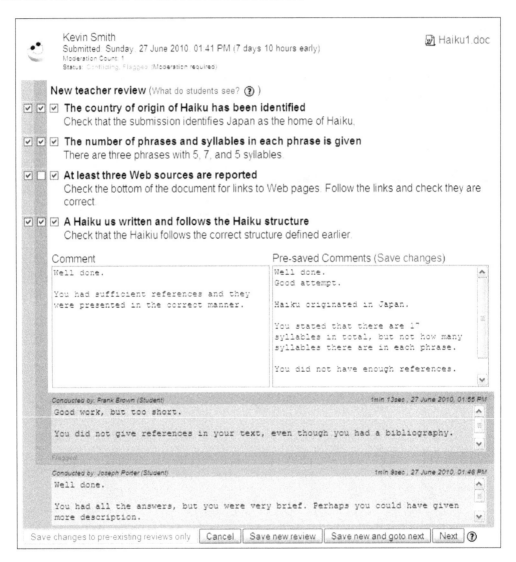

When all conflicts are resolved, and all status indicators are green, the system is able to suggest marks for all students. These can be released individually or all at once by clicking the button labeled **Set all unset calculatable grades** at the bottom of the submissions list.

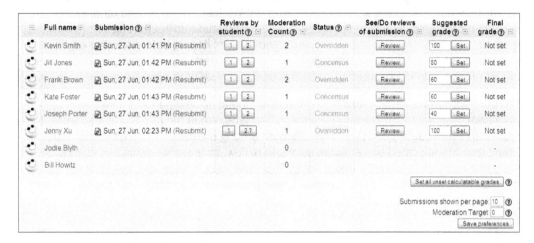

The Peer Review Assignment Type also includes an **Analysis** page which may be useful when refining an assignment for later re-use, or for teachers conducting research around assessment.

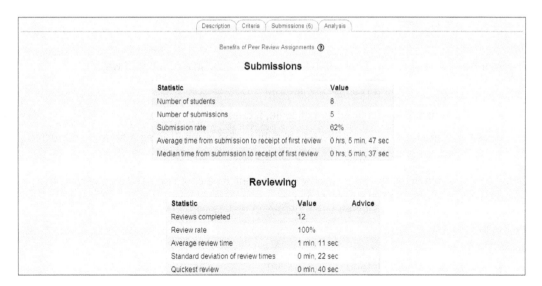

## How it works...

The Peer Review Assignment Type achieves a simpler model of peer assessment by altering the way review relationships are allocated. With the Workshop module and other peer assessment systems, a phased approach is taken, with students submitting before one deadline, waiting for relationships to be arranged, then reviewing before another deadline. Such a phased model does not leave room for late submissions, and the delay while students wait for reviews may cause them to lose track of the context of the assignment.

With the Peer Review Assignment Type, there is an initial pooling period where early submitters must wait for more submissions to be made. When the fifth student submits, this triggers an event causing reviews to be allocated among the initial pool. When later students submit they are allocated earlier submissions to review, so these students can go directly from submission to reviewing without delay. This leaves some submissions at the tail end that require teacher moderation, however it also means late submitters can simply join the tail end.

 Because of the review allocation method, only a single submission is permitted. Students are warned about this. If a student submits the wrong file, a teacher can replace their submission (and ensure the replacement is moderated).

## There's more...

The Peer Review Assignment Type can be used for teaching in a number of ways:

- As an extension of a regular assignment
- For a series of streamlined, small scale, focused assignments
- As a draft stage review before a final submission (submitted as a normal, instructor marked assignment)

Outside regular teaching, the Peer Review Assignment Type could be used for the review of research papers submitted to a conference.

## See also

- Workshop module (standard in Moodle)
- Upload PDF Assignment Type

# Recording audio for assignments

| Name | NanoGong Assignment Type |
|---|---|
| **Module type** | Assignment type |
| **Author** | Dan Poltawski |
| **Released** | 2009 |
| **Maintained** | Only barely |
| **Languages** | English, Spanish |
| **Compliance** | Good |
| **Documentation** | None |
| **Errors** | None displayed |

Have you ever wanted to break away from mundane text assignments? Well now you can allow students to submit spoken assignments instead. There have been a few attempts to allow audio recording in Moodle, but the NanoGong is the first to be truly cross-platform, while still being admirably simple.

## Getting ready

Unzip and copy the `nanogong` directory into the `/moodle/mod/assignment/type/` directory then visit the **Notifications** page.

## How to do it...

One downside to NonoGong is that it requires the Java Runtime Environment to be installed on both the teacher's machine and students' machines. Without the JRE, the NanoGong applet will not work. This can be problematic as students who are not administrators of their machines may not have the potential to install the JRE. Even if they can, the JRE is a 15 MB download, which is not huge but is still significant for students on slow, unreliable connections.

If the JRE is not installed, students might not be prompted to install the JRE. Instructions should be explicitly included with assignments on what to expect and what to do if no recorder appears.

Another problem that affects voice recording in general is the need for a microphone. It seems rather obvious, but many students will not have access to a microphone in order to record their voice.

If you are satisfied that these impediments are not significant obstacles, the NanoGong Assignment Type is worth testing. Once installed, the Assignment Type can be added from the **Add an activity...** menu, below **Assignments**.

The NanoGong Assignment Type is based on the **Upload a single file** assignment type, and is configured in the same way. It should therefore be familiar to teachers who have used that Assignment Type before.

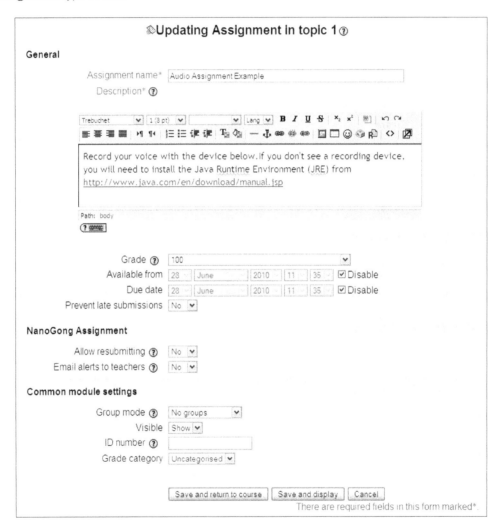

Once configured, students have access to the recorder applet. They must download the applet from the server. The .jar file for the applet is only 186 KB, so downloading should not take long. Students will then have to allow the applet to run on their machines. They have the potential to allow the applet for future occasions to skip this approval step.

Students will then see a small recorder at the bottom of the assignment description view page. Instructors can also test the recorder.

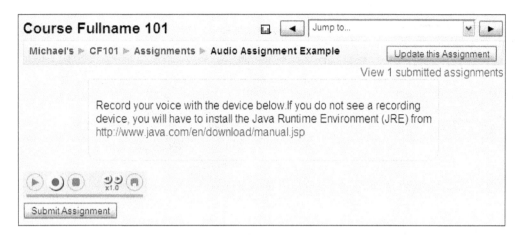

Students can record their voice, pausing when necessary. There is a five minute limit on recordings, which is demonstrated by the bar that grows across the bottom of the recorder as the five minutes passes. A reassuring VU meter fluctuates up and down next to the stop button as the user speaks. Students can play back their recording and re-record their message if they wish to. They can keep a copy of their recording by saving it to their machine as a .wav file. When they are ready, clicking the submit button allows students to submit.

The sound files created by the applet are remarkably small, so submitting the file and accessing it again afterwards takes little time. A full five minute recording produces a file around 1 MB in size; this is about 20% of an equivalent MP3 recording at CD quality.

For marking, submissions are shown in an assignments table.

The recordings are shown in the **Last modified (Student)** column. Each recording is loaded when the page loads. This is convenient if you are marking assignments using the **quick grading** feature. However, this could take time to load and consume considerable bandwidth if there is a large class and each student has submitted a five minute recording. To avoid loading each submission every time the submissions list is refreshed, hide the column that contains the recorder applet; you will still be able to access the recording from the submission single view window when marking.

## How it works...

The NanoGong Assignment Type uses the NanoGong applet created by the Hong Kong University of Science and Technology. That particular applet uses a speech codec called Speex, which targets the frequencies needed for voice. Unfortunately this means the NanoGong Assignment Type cannot be used for a broader range of frequencies, and therefore is not a good alternative for recording musical instruments, and probably not a good recorder for sung vocal performances.

## There's more...

With the potential to record voice submissions for assignments, a number of pedagogical applications open up. Here are some ideas.

- Foreign language spoken word assignments
- Poetry reading
- Simulated political speeches
- News reading practise
- Student's favorite joke

## See also

- NanoGong Activity Module (see **Modules and plugins** database)

# Replacing paper submissions

| | |
|---|---|
| **Name** | Upload PDF |
| **Module type** | Assignment Type |
| **Author** | David Smith |
| **Released** | 2009 |
| **Maintained** | Actively |
| **Languages** | English |
| **Compliance** | Good |
| **Documentation** | `readme.txt` file, help files |
| **Errors** | None displayed |

Have you ever suggested that a teacher should try electronic submission, only to be rebuffed because of a perceived need to mark paper submissions? Well, with the Upload PDF Assignment Type you can achieve the same results as "red ink on paper", plus there are a few more conveniences that will make marking go by faster. This is all achieved on the server through a web browser, without downloading files to the marker's machine.

## Getting ready

Unzip and copy the `uploadpdf` directory into the `/moodle/mod/assignment/type/` directory then visit the **Notifications** page.

The module also makes use of GhostScript to save PDFs, so you will also need to install GhostScript and direct the module to it. A download link for GhostScript is available on the Moodle **Modules and plugins** DB entry page for the Upload PDF Assignment Type.

If you are using Windows, be sure to install GhostScript to a location so that its path contains no spaces, for example, `C:\gs`. Once installed you need to write the path to the GhostScript executable into `uploadpdf_config.php` located in the module directory. The first line of code appears as...

```
$CFG->gs_path = 'gs';
```

...and needs to be changed to include the path to the GhostScript executable, for example:

```
$CFG->gs_path = 'C:\gs\gs8.71\bin\gswin32c.exe';
```

## How to do it...

Once the module is installed and GhostScript is set up, you can add an assignment by selecting the **Upload PDF** option from the **Add an activity...** menu, below **Assignments**.

The configuration page for an UploadPDF assignment begins with the same **General** settings as other Assignment Types. This includes a name, description, grade value, and due date.

In the description, you may want to include instructions about converting files to PDF format. OpenOffice offers native support for saving to PDF. An add-on can be installed for Office2007 (and later versions) to "publish" to PDF. GoogleDocs allows files to be saved as PDF. There are online services that can convert documents to PDF, some of which are free (but may involve limitations or complications). For general applications, it is possible to install a PDF printer, which masquerades as a printer, but instead of printing to a physical device, it produces a PDF file which can be saved to disk. A number of PDF printer solutions are freely available and simple to install.

 The requirement for students to produce a PDF file is a limitation. Students may be working on machines where they are not the administrator and may not have the privileges to install a PDF printer or an add-on. If that is the case, you may have to provide independent assistance to students to help them convert their submissions to PDF.

Below the **General** settings there are some specific settings for an **Upload PDF** assignment.

**Upload PDF**

| | |
|---|---|
| Coversheet ⑦ | [_____] [Choose or upload a file ...] |
| Template ⑦ | [None ▼] |
| | [Edit Templates...] |
| Maximum size | [1MB ▼] |
| All files must be PDFs ⑦ | [Yes ▼] |
| Allow deleting ⑦ | [Yes ▼] |
| Maximum number of uploaded files ⑦ | [3 ▼] |
| Allow notes ⑦ | [No ▼] |
| Hide description before available date ⑦ | [No ▼] |
| Email alerts to teachers ⑦ | [No ▼] |

If your institution has a standard coversheet that needs to be fixed to all submissions, this coversheet can be supplied (in PDF format of course) and will be prefixed to students' submissions.

Controls can be placed on the files students submit. It is likely you will want to restrict submissions to PDF format, unless you want students to submit an accompanying file with their PDF. Students can submit more than one file. Each PDF file they submit is concatenated into a single document as it arrives at the server, so a single document is presented when marking.

Help files are available here to explain each setting.

With the assignment in place, students submit their PDF files in much the same way they would submit using other assignment types. The Upload PDF Assignment Type offers a two-staged submission. First students must submit each individual file. Once all the files are sent to the Moodle server, the student completes and confirms their submission, making it available for marking.

When assignments have been submitted, the teacher can mark from the assignments list.

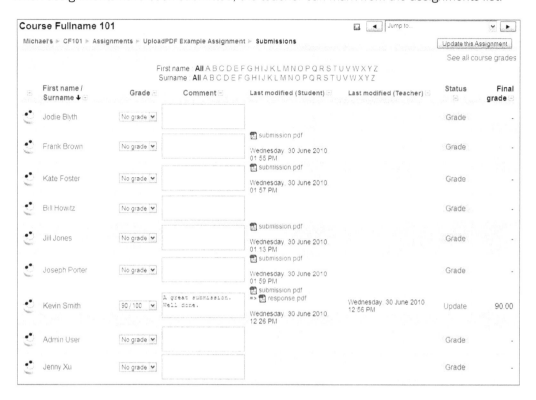

The module author recommends marking with the **Allow quick grading** preference turned on. This makes sense as the PDFs are annotated in a separated window, so using grading windows means a lot of open windows. If you are using this Assignment Type it is likely that most of your feedback will be in the PDF itself, so adding a mark and a short overall comment on the assignments list page is probably sufficient.

To annotate a submission, click on the **submission.pdf** link. This opens a new window with a student's combined submission, visible page by page.

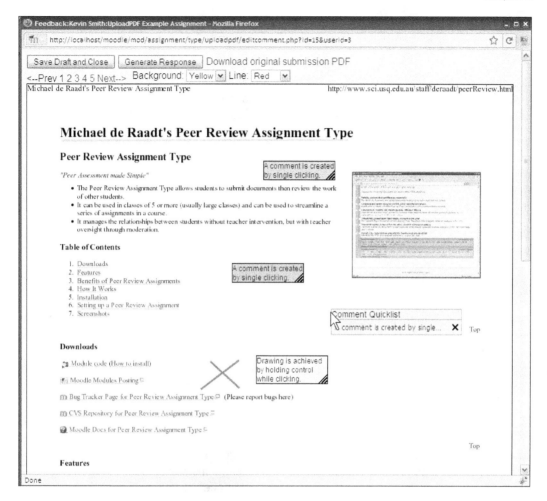

In this window, a teacher can annotate a student's submission. Comments can be started by left-clicking on the document. A comment box will appear and text can be inserted; when editing is complete, click off the comment. If you wish to edit a comment, clicking on the comment will allow you to change the text inside. Right-clicking on a comment will allow you to control background color. It is also possible to save comments to the **Comment Quicklist** by right-clicking on a comment and selecting **Add to Comment Quicklist**. This is particularly useful when marking a large number of submissions as it saves retyping repeated comments. To use a comment from the Quicklist, simply right-click where you want the comment to appear and choose the comment from the list.

You can also add lines to the document to indicate where corrections need to be made, or to add emphasis. To draw a line, or more than one, hold the *Ctrl* key, then click-and-drag the mouse.

Changes are saved as you make them, so if you close the window, your changes will reappear when you come back. You can also click the button labeled **Save Draft and Close** for the same effect. A teacher can move from page to page, adding comments and lines as they go.

It should be noted that a document including a teacher's annotations will not be made available to the student until you click **Generate Response**. The "response" is a new document, based on the submitted document, and including the annotations created by a teacher. Once created, a student can download this response document from their view of the assignment.

Back at the submissions list, the teacher can add a general comment and set a mark, then save the marks by clicking **Save all my feedback** at the bottom of the list.

## How it works...

The response document is produced very efficiently. It is not a bitmap capture (like a digital photograph) of the document with annotations. It is effectively the original PDF document with annotations as vector (drawing) objects. All original text and graphics are preserved after the addition of these new objects. These new objects add only a very small amount to the original file size.

## There's more...

In general, assignment feedback can be classified as structured or unstructured. The Upload PDF Assignment Type is an ingenious solution to providing unstructured feedback in an online environment, especially as there are no documents that need to be transferred back and forth between the server and the teacher's machine.

The pedagogical applications are wide open:

- Essays (of course)
- Reports
- Poetry
- Artworks
- Journal articles
- ...and effectively anything that can become a PDF

## See also

▸    Peer Review Assignment Type

# Allowing students to contribute to assessment

| Name | Question Creation Module |
|---|---|
| **Module type** | Activity |
| **Author** | Jamie Pratt |
| **Released** | 2008 |
| **Maintained** | Actively |
| **Languages** | English, Spanish |
| **Compliance** | Good |
| **Documentation** | Limited online documentation, help files |
| **Errors** | Some errors displayed when error reporting is turned on |

The Question Creation Module allows students to contribute Quiz questions and be rewarded with marks. This is a great pedagogical activity and the questions produced by students can be used in creative ways.

## Getting ready

Unzip and copy the module directory into the `/moodle/mod/` directory then visit the **Notifications** page.

## How to do it...

After adding the Question Creation Module you can create an instance of this activity from the **Add an activity...** menu.

The configuration page for this module is somewhat overcomplicated, however, once you have used it, the settings become apparent.

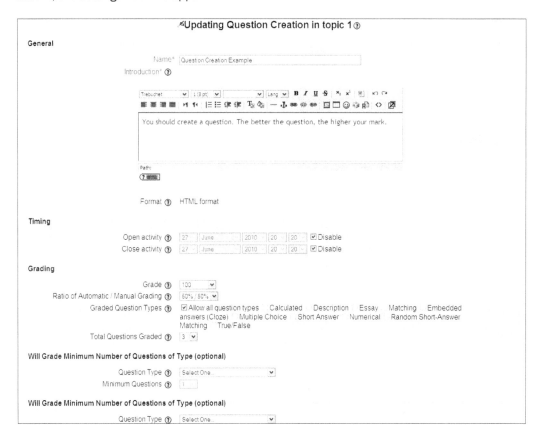

Like most modules, there is a **Name**. There is also a description that appears as an **Introduction** to students in their view of the activity. A time period for the activity can be specified with an opening and closing date.

In the **Grading** section, there are a number of options, some of which are obvious and some that require explanation. A Question Creation activity can contribute to a course assessment and as such there is a **Grade** value. This grade value is constituted from a mix of:

▸ Automatic grading (based on number of questions created by a student, that is, a participation mark)

▸ Manual grading (based on a judgment of quality by the teacher

A 50%/50% mix means that the student gains half the available marks by simply creating the required number of questions and the other half based on the judgment of the teacher. A different ratio can be chose to shift this balance depending on the teacher's preference. For a fully automated assessment, a ratio of 100%/0% can be used. For a grade that is wholly based on the teacher's judgment a ratio of 0%/100% can be used.

The number of questions that need to be created can be specified. The grade value is then distributed across this number of questions.

The types of Quiz questions can be restricted to specific types or students can be allowed to create questions of any type. The teacher can direct that the student create a minimum number of questions of specified question types. For example, the teacher could direct that two of the questions that a student creates should be **Multiple Choice**. Such enforcement is achieved in the sections labeled (rather incomprehensibly) as **Will Grade Minimum Number of Questions of Type (optional)**.

At the bottom of the configuration page, there is a setting that controls what level of editing students have over their own questions.

It is not clear at first what each level of access means, nor why access needs to be restricted. Students can be controlled in their freedom to create, preview, edit, and delete questions. The module author suggests that there may be complications if a student edits a question after it has been graded, although he also suggests that students could improve questions based on feedback and such questions could then be re-graded (and the module facilitates this). For the most intuitive setup for students, the highest level of access is probably best. The teacher could then grade the questions after a set deadline. In a two phased approach that allows questions to be improved, questions could be checked at a specified date, with final question edits required by the set deadline.

Students have an interface to launch the question creation process. When a question type is selected, students then create a question of that type using the same interface that a teacher uses when they create questions for a quiz.

---

You should create a question. The better the question, the higher your mark.

**Activity is open.** No time limits set.

## Required Questions to Create

- **You've done 3 extra questions. 3 questions of any of the types below will be graded**
  - Calculated
  - Description
  - Essay
  - Matching
  - Embedded answers (Cloze)
  - Multiple Choice You've done one question of this type.
    - JavaScript description *(70/100)"A bit too basic."*🔍✎✗
  - Short Answer You've done 2 questions of this type.
    - Source code *(70/100)"A good question, but not too well written."*🔍✎✗
    - Array index *(80/100)"A great question."*🔍✎✗
  - Numerical
  - Random Short-Answer Matching
  - True/False
- *You have been awarded a total grade of 86.67 / 100 for this activity.*
  - *You have been awarded an automatic grade of 50 / 50 for these questions, since you have done 3 of 3 required questions.*
  - *A teacher has awarded you a grade of 36.66667 / 50 for the questions you have done.*

---

Students can create more than the required number of questions. Their final mark is based on the best questions they have created.

Questions created by students appear in a list much like an assignments submission table.

In this view, a teacher can preview a question and grade it. They can also provide comments on each question. The final grade is calculated when the teacher clicks the button at the bottom of this page labeled **Save all grades & feedback**. Grades are calculated according to how many of the required questions a student has created and the quality of each question. The student's final grade is the calculated value across all of their questions.

## How it works...

Questions created by students are stored in the Moodle Question Bank. In that form they can be used by teachers in the course like any other question in the Question Bank.

## There's more...

Requiring students to create questions is a great learning exercise. It forces students to think about the course materials at a higher level in order to form questions that someone else will find challenging.

The real possibilities of this activity fall not in what the students can create, but in what the teacher can do with the questions that students have made. Here are some ideas:

► Using the best questions for regular quizzes (keeping in mind that at least one student will already know the answer)

- ▶ Using the best questions for quizzes for a successive cohort
- ▶ Using student created questions as the basis for a final exam

# Getting more out of quizzes

| Name | Drag-and-drop matching question type, |
| --- | --- |
| | Drag-and-drop ordering question type, |
| | Image target question type |
| **Module type** | Question type |
| **Author** | Adriane Boyd |
| **Released** | 2007 |
| **Maintained** | Actively |
| **Languages** | English, German, Japanese, Russian |
| **Compliance** | Good |
| **Documentation** | Design documentation, `readme.txt` file |
| **Errors** | None displayed |

Automated assessment can be used to complement other assessment mechanisms, or in some cases, to replace it entirely. Moodle offers the Quiz module for automated assessment and quizzes can contain a variety of different types of questions. In line with Moodle's principle of modularity, it is possible to add new question types to this mix. Here are a few good examples.

## Getting ready

Unzip and copy the question type directories into the `/moodle/question/type/` directory, then visit the **Notifications** page.

## How to do it...

You can add questions directly to the question bank to be added to quizzes later, or you can add questions as you are developing a quiz. To create questions in the question bank, click on **Questions** in the **Administration** block on a course page.

In the question bank, you can add new questions by selecting a question type from the list labeled **Create new question**.

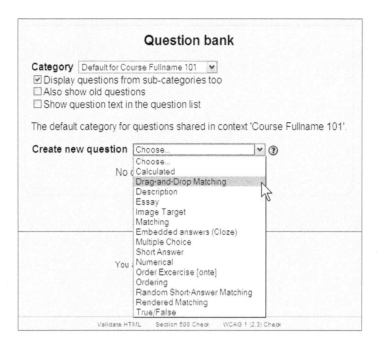

The Drag-and-drop matching question type is an extension of the regular matching question type. It relies on JavaScript to allow students to drag together matching items, but falls back to the functionality of the regular matching question if JavaScript is not turned on. It is a pretty safe bet that you can rely on students having JavaScript turned on, so it is likely they will get the most out of this question type.

Selecting **Drag-and-Drop Matching** from the **Create a new question** menu will launch the creation of a new question of this type. All question types have the same **General** settings.

Enter a name for the question and the question text, then scroll down.

For a Drag-and-drop matching question, you must supply at least three pairings. The nomenclature for pairings is slightly odd. Each pairing is grouped as **Question 1**, **Question 2**, and so on:

For each pairing there is a **Question** and an **Answer**. When the question is displayed, the list of **Question** text labels will appear on the left and the matching **Answer** text labels will appear, in shuffled order, on the right. Adding a pairing without a **Question** label adds an **Answer** label that will not be matched. This is useful for adding distracters to the quiz question.

The Drag-and-drop ordering question type allows questions to be created that require students to put a list of items into the correct order.

Selecting **Ordering** from the **Create a new question** menu will launch the creation of a new question of this type. Again there are general settings that must be entered. Add a question name. You may also want to add question text that gives the context of the items and prompts the user to reorder the items.

Below the general settings, the items to be ordered need to be specified. The items should be entered in the correct order; they will be shuffled each time the question appears to a student.

Available choices  You must provide at least three items in the correct order. Entries where the item is blank will be ignored.

Display items horizontally ☐

Item 1

> Tuesday

Item 2

> Wednesday

Item 3

> Thursday

Item 4

> Friday

Item 5

There is also an option to **Display the items horizontally**. With this option checked, the items will appear side-by-side, which would be appropriate for a short list of items with brief labels. Leaving this option unchecked causes the items to appear in a vertical list.

The Image target question type allows the teacher to upload an image containing areas that can be identified. The student must drag a target onto the correct area (or one of a number of specified areas) to answer the question correctly.

Before adding an Image target question, you should upload an image to the course files area. Click on **Files** in the course **Administration** area. In **Files**, click on the button labeled **Upload a file** and you will be presented with a form containing a file browse box. Click **Browse** and a file dialog box will appear. Locate the image file (it should have a .jpg extension) and select it. Back at the **Upload a file** form, click on the button labeled **Upload this file** and, after the file is uploaded, it should appear in the files area. With the file in place, you can then create an Image Target question that makes use of it.

Selecting **Image Target** from the **Create a new question** menu will launch the creation of a new question of this type. In the **General** settings, add a question name and question text that prompts the user to drag the target onto the identifiable item.

Below the general settings, there is a drop-down list labeled **Question image**. Opening the list will reveal the images in the course directory that can be selected. Select the image you have uploaded and click on **Insert image to specify answer**.

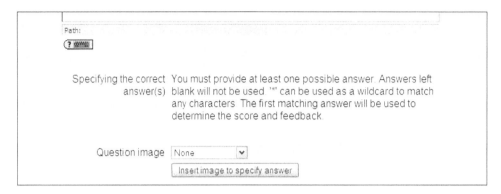

The page will reload and the chosen image will appear.

You must now specify the area within the image that, if identified by the student, will be seen as a correct answer. On top of the image there is a semi-transparent mask and within this there is a resizable area. The area can be moved by clicking and dragging it. It can also be resized by dragging the handles around the edges of the image. It is possible to add more target areas if needed.

## How it works...

The Drag-and-drop matching question type provides a far more intuitive interface for identifying matches, compared to the regular matching interface. This would be particularly useful for assessing younger students.

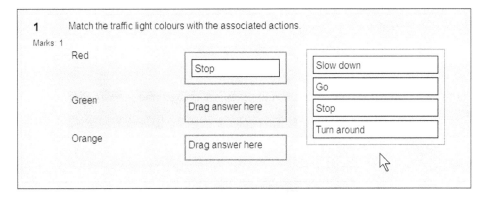

To answer the question, a student must drag the options from the right on to the target locations on the left, next to the appropriate label. Students can drag questions off the targets or replace answers with another.

Answer correctness is not displayed in the teacher preview of the question, but it does appear when a student answers the quiz.

A Drag-and-drop order question appears with the items appearing in shuffled order. The student must drag items to their correct position. When an item is moved, other items make way by moving around it. The end result is a very intuitive way of ordering items.

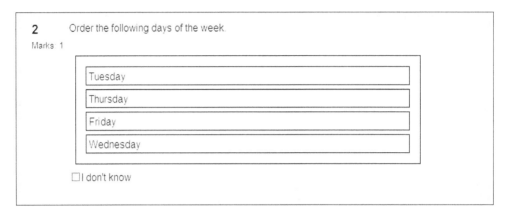

The Image target question type appears with the question text above an image, and a cross-hair target to the left.

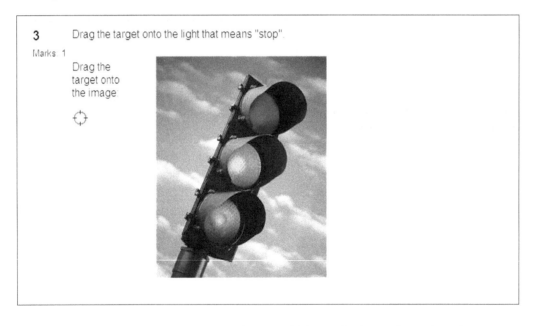

The student must drag the target onto the image, within the designated area in order to achieve a correct answer.

## There's more...

These new question types open up a number of new teaching applications. The Drag-and-drop matching question could be used for:

- Matching injuries to first-aid treatments
- Matching inventors to their inventions
- Matching sports stars to their sports or movie stars to their movies

Drag-and-drop order questions could be used with information that falls into a sequence.

- Ordering the atomic mass of particles
- Ordering steps in biological process
- Ordering statements in a computer program so it will produce a correct output

The Image target question type can be used to ask students to locate items visually.

- Identifying locations on a map
- Identifying specific people in a group photograph
- Playing "Where's Wally"/"Where's Waldo", perhaps adapted to a particular teaching context, for example, "Where's Einstein"

## See also

- QuizPort module (see **Modules and plugins** database)

# Giving immediate formative feedback

| Name | Hidden Text |
|---|---|
| **Module type** | Filter |
| **Author** | Dmitry Pupinin |
| **Released** | 2008 |
| **Maintained** | Limited |
| **Languages** | English, French, German, Hebrew, Japanese, Russian |
| **Compliance** | Good |
| **Documentation** | Online documentation |
| **Errors** | None displayed |

The main aim of assessment is to encourage student learning. Not all assessment needs to be worth marks and not all assessment needs to be large scale. The Hidden Text filter allows hidden text to be included in and around a Moodle site. This can be used to prompt students to anticipate answers and then reveal them to confirm their suspicions and reinforce their learning.

## Getting ready

Unzip and copy the `hiddentext` directory into the `/moodle/filter/` directory then navigate to **Site Administration | Modules | Filters | Manage Filters** and click on the eye icon in the row labeled **Hiddentext**.

## How to do it...

With the filter in place, text can be marked as hidden text by placing filter tags around it. In a WYSIWYG editor `[span]` and `[div]` tags can be used. A `[span]` tag can be used within a sentence and a `[div]` tag hides a section of a paragraph or more.

If you wanted to ask a question and temporarily hide the answer you could write content as follows:

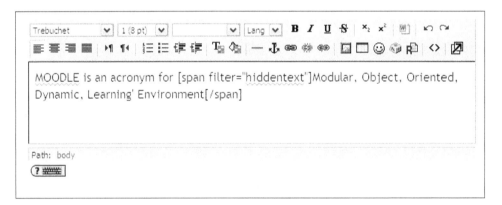

Before the hidden content there is a filter tag:

`[span filter="hidden text"]`

The end of the hidden content is followed by a closing filter tag:

`[/span]`

When the text is parsed by the filter, the hidden text is replaced by an eye icon.

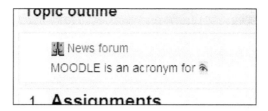

Clicking on the icon reveals the hidden text.

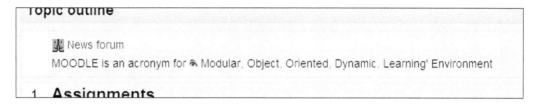

Clicking the icon again re-hides the content.

The icon itself is meaningful, but not necessarily intuitive. It is possible to add a label to accompany the icon. This is achieved by adding a `desc` attribute to the initial filter tag.

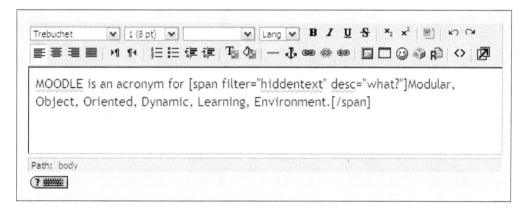

The label is then rendered next to the icon as follows.

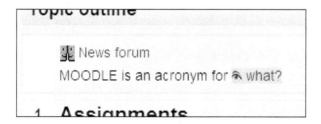

## How it works...

The Hidden Text filter uses the YUI library to hide and reveal text. This is how it achieves a fade effect.

## There's more...

The Hidden Text filter is not limited to questions and answers. It can be used to hide content of any kind. Here are some applications:

- Hiding additional information that, if shown in the original view, might overcomplicate the content for most readers

- Inserting links that do not distract from the flow of the content, but can be revealed if needed

- Placing "Easter eggs" or secret information around the site to encourage students to explore

# Recognizing high performers

| Name | Course Results |
|---|---|
| **Module type** | Block |
| **Author** | Vlas Voloshin |
| **Released** | 2009 |
| **Maintained** | Limited |
| **Languages** | English, Russian |
| **Compliance** | Good |
| **Documentation** | `readme.txt` file |
| **Errors** | None displayed |

There's something to be said about a little competition to motivate students. Informing students about the top performers in a course, allows them to have an accurate understanding of their success in the course. The Course Results block allows a teacher to show the best (and worst) results from any marked activity within a course, or category grades, or even the course total.

## Getting ready

Unzip and copy the block directory into the `/moodle/blocks/` directory then visit the **Notifications** page.

## How to do it...

In the **Blocks** list, the Course Results block is listed as **Results**. When a block is initially added it will present a message encouraging you to update it.

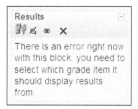

Clicking on the configuration icon takes you to the configuration page.

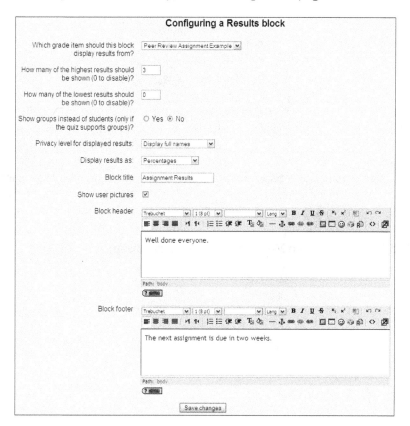

The first choice you need to make is the grade item you want to display in the Course Results block. If you want to show the overall course results, you can choose **Course Total**. You need to specify a number of highest or lowest results; you can't leave both of these as zero. Unless you are a ruthless teacher, unafraid of litigation, you would not want to reveal the identity of your poorest performing students, so you will more than likely want to set a number for the highest results.

You can choose if names and pictures are shown with results. Result values can be given as percentages, fractions (for example, 80/100) or as numeric marks.

The block title can be set, which allows you to have multiple blocks for different results. You can also provide text to appear before and after the results list.

## How it works...

The block shows the top results in a table.

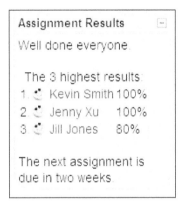

The table updates automatically based on the latest results each time the page is loaded.

## See also

▸ Quiz Results block (see **Modules and plugins** database)

# 7
# Organizing Students

In this chapter, we will cover:

- ▸ Student nominated groups
- ▸ Identifying peers
- ▸ Helping with time management
- ▸ Getting feedback

## Introduction

So you have a flashy collection of wonderful material, arranged efficiently, and assessed accurately. How can you ensure that students are involved and interacting with each other in a course?

This chapter brings together a loose collection of modules that will aid you to create harmonious student groups, allow users to be identified by relationship, help students manage their time, and get students to tell you what they thought of the whole experience.

### Student nominated groups

Putting students into groups is useful, particularly when group projects need to be completed. However, placing students in groups can be fraught with problems, one of which is unhappy students wanting to be shuffled into another group after a personality clash. With self-nominated groups, students take on the responsibility for choosing which group they will belong to.

- ▸ Group selection module

## Identifying peers

Within Moodle, there are many relationships that can exist between users holding different roles; students can have teachers and group-mates, and teachers can have students, fellow teachers, markers, and administrators. Keeping track of who holds these roles can be aided by one simple, flexible block.

- ▶ My peers block

## Helping with time management

Learning management systems allow a greater variety of activities than has been possible with traditional forms of education. With assignments, quizzes, forum discussions, materials to read and other activities to complete, it's easy for students to lose track of what they have done and what they need to do next. Helping students manage their time will assist them to complete tasks, and hopefully to stay with the course. This is the focus of one block.

- ▶ Progress Bar block

## Getting feedback

So you've been trying some new, dazzling approaches to teaching and you want to know what the students think about it. Moodle provides some fixed educational surveys, but they are unlikely to ask the questions you really want answered. Well, there is a module that allows you to create the survey you want.

- ▶ Feedback module

# Allowing students to form groups

| | |
|---|---|
| **Name** | Group selection |
| **Module Type** | Activity module |
| **Author** | Petr Skoda, Helen Foster, David Mudrak, Anna Vanova |
| **Released** | 2009 |
| **Maintained** | Actively |
| **Languages** | English |
| **Compliance** | Good |
| **Documentation** | Limited online documentation, `Readme.txt` file |
| **Errors** | None displayed |

Breaking students into groups allows teachers to manage students in smaller numbers. Putting students into groups permits them to interact on a smaller scale. The concepts of groups can be applied to most activities around a Moodle course.

One of the downsides to groups is the tedious business of placing students into groups they will be happy with. There are the usual requests for a student to be grouped with a friend. There is also the hassle of accommodating late starters or reorganizing groups after a student "drops out".

The Group selection module enables students to "enroll" in groups of their own. The module works with the group functionality that is already baked into Moodle, and works well.

 The Group selection module began its life in 2004 with Moodle 1.4. It has changed hands among multiple authors over the period since. Despite this, it is now a simple, well designed module.

## Getting ready

Unzip and copy the `groupselect` directory into the `/moodle/mod/` directory then visit the **Notifications** page.

## How to do it...

Once installed, the Group selection module is created as an activity by selecting it from the **Add an activity...** list. The module's configuration page should appear as follows.

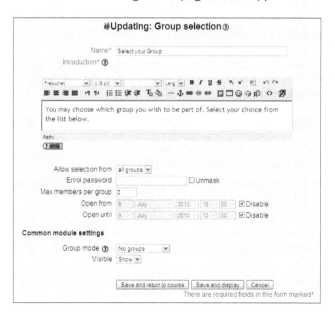

The **Name** and **Introduction** settings should be used to instruct students about how they should choose a group. The **Name** appears as a link to the Group selection module on the course page, so it should be directive. The **Introduction** appears above the facility to choose a group so it can be used as instructive text for students. The module allows some restriction of group size and which groups can be selected, but you may want to include instructions on other rules that students must follow when creating their groups. For example, you may want groups to have a mix of male and female students, or you may want to encourage students to work with students they don't normally associate with; such rules could be expressed in the introductory text.

After the first two settings, there are some options to control how and when students can join groups. The setting labeled **Allow selection from** allows the teacher to restrict which groups students may join. You must define the groups you wish to allow inside a grouping which can be selected from this list. If you don't have groupings or don't want to restrict which groups students can join, leave this setting as the default for **all groups**.

Groupings are clusters of groups. Sometimes you may wish to allow members of different groups to interact, so a grouping can be created that combines groups. Groupings came about with version 1.9, but they are turned off by default. You can turn them on at **Administration | Miscellaneous | Experimental | Enable groupings** (although groupings are not really experimental any more). Once enabled, you can create groupings and populate them with groups on the **Groupings** tab in the **Groups** settings page for a course. More information is available at `http://docs.moodle.org/en/Groupings`.

A password can be set that restricts which students can use the facility to join a group. If you only wish to allow specific students in a course to enroll in groups you could provide only those students with the password. This may be particularly useful on open sites with self enrolment, where you want to restrict groups to specific people.

You can set a maximum size for each group. Leaving this at zero removes the size restriction, in other words, allowing groups to grow to any size.

A time period when students can join groups can be specified by creating an opening and/or closing date.

Under **Common module settings** there are two configuration options. These appear because they are included on the configuration pages of all activity modules. Having the **Group mode** and other advanced group options here may confuse some teachers

## How it works...

When the module is set up, students can use it to **Enroll** in the group they wish to join.

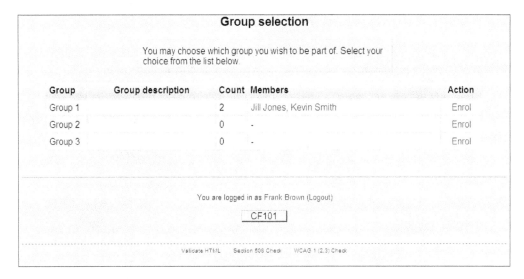

While enrolling they can view the profiles of the members already enrolled in each group. This may be helpful when students are unfamiliar with other students in the course.

Once in a group, students can **Unenroll** and join another group.

A teacher can see the result of students enrolling in groups:

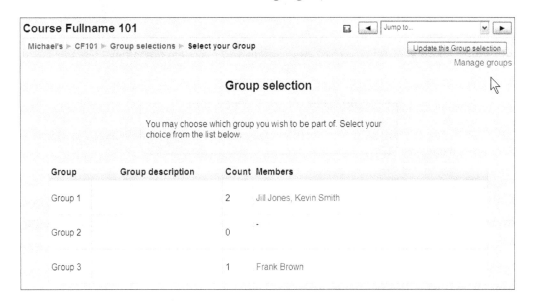

If a teacher wishes to affect changes to the membership of groups, they can use the standard group management facility. There is a handy link at the top right corner to access this facility, when it is viewed by a teacher or administrator.

## There's more...

The use of groups can have many applications in teaching settings. By allowing students to self-nominate their group membership, a number of new opportunities arise:

▶ Forming project groups with students selecting the project they wish to work on

▶ Interest clubs who can have forums and Wiki space for discussions and collecting information about their topic of interest

▶ Research collaborations for higher education courses or where Moodle is used as a content management system in a research setting

# Identifying people

| Name | My peers |
|---|---|
| **Module type** | Block |
| **Author** | Étienne Rozé |
| **Released** | 2009 |
| **Maintained** | Actively |
| **Languages** | English, French, Hebrew |
| **Compliance** | OK |
| **Documentation** | Online documentation |
| **Errors** | Warnings displayed with error reporting turned on. |

The My peers block was originally called the My Teachers block. The block can still be used to show details of teachers to students, but with the advent of Moodle's new flexible role system, the block can now be used to identify people involved in a course, based on many different relationships.

## Getting ready

Unzip and copy the `my_peers` directory into the `/moodle/blocks/` directory then visit the **Notifications** page.

## How to do it...

When installed, an instance of the block can be added to a course page by turning editing on and choosing "**My peers**" from the **Blocks** menu.

By default, the block is designed to show a list of teachers and their details to students. If this is all you want the block to do, you don't have to configure the block any further, although there are a number of settings you might want to change (for example, the block title).

Examining the settings in the block configuration page will allow you to see the variety of uses this block can be used to achieve.

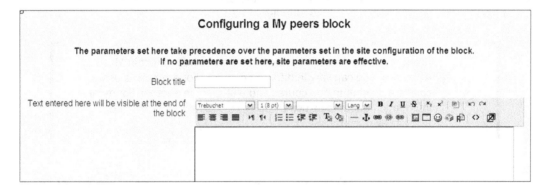

At the top of the configuration page there is a notice that signifies there are global settings for this block. At the global level the same configuration settings are present, except for the role matrix (explained later). The message indicates that global settings will be used unless they are overridden by instance settings. It's not clear why this message needs to be there as teachers who are not administrators cannot access the global settings anyway.

The first setting allows a teacher to name the block. Considering the variety of applications, and the generic nature of the default block title, it is likely you will want to set a more appropriate title.

You can add text in the block to appear below the list of users. This might be useful for specifying additional information, for example, contact timings or rules for contacting users.

| | | Administrator | Course creator | Teacher | Non-editing teacher | Student | Guest |
|---|---|---|---|---|---|---|---|
| Choose here whom (in row) can see whom (in column) | Administrator | ☐ | ☐ | ☐ | ☐ | ☐ | ☐ |
| | Course creator | ☐ | ☐ | ☐ | ☐ | ☐ | ☐ |
| | Teacher | ☐ | ☐ | ☐ | ☐ | ☐ | ☐ |
| | Non-editing teacher | ☐ | ☐ | ☐ | ☐ | ☐ | ☐ |
| | Student | ☐ | ☑ | ☑ | ☑ | ☐ | ☐ |
| | Guest | ☐ | ☐ | ☐ | ☐ | ☐ | ☐ |

Below this is a matrix of users. The matrix is based on the roles used in the course. If there have been additional roles added to your site, or if the role names have been re-titled, your matrix will appear differently. However, regardless of the appearance, the matrix is used in the same way. Considering the roles in the course, you can specify which users are included in the list, and to who the list should appear. The users that the list will appear to are listed on the left side of the matrix. The users that appear in the list are identified by the roles listed across the top. Looking at the default example, ticks appear in the **Student** row. This indicates that the block will show a list of users to students. In that row there are ticks under **Course creator**, **Teacher**, and **Non-editing teacher**, which indicates that students will able to see a list of users in the course who have those details.

Roles provide a flexible way to control how users interact in Moodle. A person's role can vary in different courses. For example, a user can be a teacher in one course and a student in another. For more information about roles see `http://docs.moodle.org/en/ Roles_and_capabilities`.

| | |
|---|---|
| Only people in the same group will be visible. This parameter is ignored if the course setting forces the use (or not) of groups. | Yes ▼ |
| Roles are shown | Yes ▼ |
| Other contact information is shown (if activated) | No ▼ |
| A photo is shown | Yes ▼ |
| Photo size | Choose... ▼ |
| | Save changes |

Below the users matrix there are some more settings. The first setting relates to groups. One use for the block is to show a list of members in a student's own group. With this setting set to **Yes**, students are able to see other students, but only members of their own group.

The second setting controls whether or not the role name of each displayed person, such as Teacher, Student, and so on, is shown. Below this, the third setting controls what contact links are shown with a user, for example, a link to e-mail the user, visit their homepage or call the user using Skype, depending on if these details are available in the user's profile.

The final two settings control whether or not profile pictures are shown and what size of image is used. With the control to show or display images, there is also an option that, when selected, will show images only, hiding names and other details.

## How it works...

With the flexibility provided by the users matrix, and the other settings that can be changed, a variety of applications emerge in courses large or small, with or without groups.

A list of teachers in the course:

A student's group-mates:

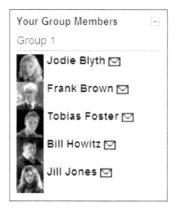

Everyone in the course:

It is also possible to mix combinations of roles in a single instance of this block. For example, teachers could see students while students can see teachers. "Tutors" of a group (assuming such a role is created) could see their own group while the "Teacher" of the course could see all students. With the potential to create roles, and the adaptability of the roles matrix in this module, the possibilities are quite numerous.

## See also

> ► Participant Pix block (see the Moodle **Modules and plugins** database)

# Time managing students

| Name | Progress Bar |
|---|---|
| **Module Type** | Block |
| **Author** | Michael de Raadt |
| **Released** | 2009 |
| **Maintained** | Actively |
| **Languages** | Dutch, English, German, Japanese, Portuguese Brazilian |
| **Compliance** | Good |
| **Documentation** | Online documentation, help files |
| **Errors** | None displayed |

In a course with a large number of tasks to undertake, students can lose track of what activities and resources need to be attempted or viewed next. The Progress Bar block aims to show students what they have attempted and what they still have to complete. Progress is indicated by segments in a bar, with each segment representing a single activity or resource, and each color-coded to show if it has been attempted. The segments are ordered chronologically to show the order that activities/resources should be attempted, and an indication of the current point in time is given.

## Getting ready

Unzip and copy the block directory into the `/moodle/blocks/` directory then visit the **Notifications** page.

## How to do it...

Once installed you can add a **Progress Bar** block from the **Blocks** menu. Initially the block appears with a message prompting the teacher to indicate which activities and/or resources should be shown in the Progress Bar.

It is assumed that you already have created activities and resources in your course. When you click on the configuration icon you are taken to a page that lists each of the activities and resources in your course.

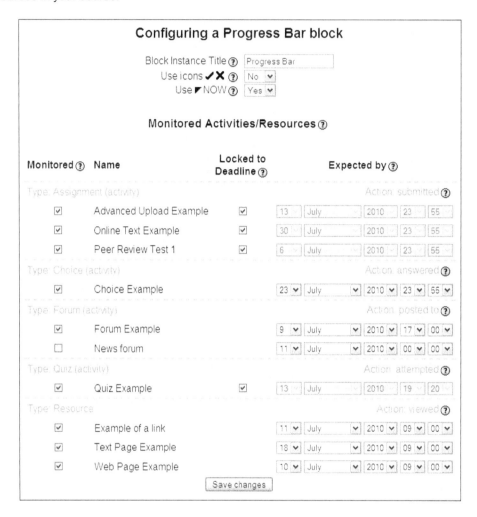

At the top of the configuration page, there are three settings. The first setting allows a teacher to change the block title from the default **Progress Bar** to some other name. If the block is used to indicate progress in a particular type of activity, say assignments, then the block could be used to show progress for just that. If that were the case, using a title like "Assignments Submitted" may provide more information. It is possible to have more than one Progress Bar block on a page with each used to show progress in different activities, and each titled appropriately.

The second setting adds tick or cross icons to Progress Bar segments. Adding these symbols provides another level of meaning to the color-coded bar segments. This may be useful if students in a class are known to be color-blind, or if the red and green colors used are not indicative of good or bad in the cultural setting of the course.

 Segment colors in the Progress Bar can be altered to match cultural meanings, or to match themes. This is accomplished using the global configuration settings for the block at **Site Administration | Modules | Blocks | Progress Bar.**

By default, the block adds an indication of the current point in time above the bar. If ordering is not relevant in a course, or if the course is not conducted over a specific time-frame, this indicator can be turned off.

The remaining settings relate to activities and resources in the course. The block is designed to work with all standard activities and resources. The commonly used Feedback and Book modules are also included. Activities and resources are grouped together in kind; for example, all assignments are grouped together. For each activity there is an expected level of involvement labeled **Action**, which is indicated on the right hand side of each group heading. This action indicates what students are expected to do in order to notionally make an attempt. With assignments students need to submit in order to turn the relative Progress Bar segment green.

Next to each activity there is a checkbox that, when enabled, includes the activity in the displayed Progress Bar. If an activity is checked, but hidden in the course, it will not appear in the Progress Bar. This is useful if a scheduled release of work is achieved by revealing hidden activities and resources as the course progresses; as activities selected in the configuration are unhidden, they will automatically appear in the Progress Bar.

Some activities, such as assignments and quizzes, can have a due date associated with them. If a due date is set, that date is used as information for the ordering of segments in the Progress Bar. These due dates can be overridden if the teacher wishes to do so. For activities and resources that do not have a due date set, the teacher must supply a date and time that it is expected to be attempted by.

## How it works...

With activities and resources selected, the Progress Bar appears to students indicating their progress in the course.

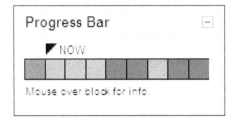

The display will differ for each student, depending on what they have accomplished this far. Segments colored red indicate a task that has past and is yet to be attempted; green indicates that an attempt has been made and blue shows tasks that have not been attempted, but are expected in the future.

When a student moves their mouse over a segment of the Progress Bar, the block expands and reveals information about the related task.

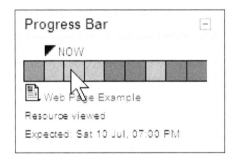

Students can click on a block segment or the name of the activity to be taken to it.

## There's more...

This block has been evaluated in teaching settings. An interesting discovery was that students felt compelled to "make the bar all green". Thanks to the operant conditioning of websites like Facebook, teachers now have another mechanism to encourage course progress.

# Surveying students

| Name | Feedback |
|---|---|
| **Module Type** | Module |
| **Author** | Andreas Grabs |
| **Released** | 2006 |
| **Maintained** | Actively |
| **Languages** | Czech, Dutch, English, Basque, Finnish, French, German, Italian, Japanese, Polish, Portuguese Brazilian, Slovak, Spanish, Swedish |
| **Compliance** | Good |
| **Documentation** | Online documentation, Readme.txt file, Help files |
| **Errors** | None displayed |

Have you ever wanted to survey students, using the Survey module, but found that it does not ask the questions you want to ask? The standard Survey module allows teachers to use specific, validated surveys that assess teaching in a course; it is inflexible and not customizable. The Feedback module, however, is completely customizable and well implemented also.

There are two modules that can be used to survey students in Moodle. One is the Feedback module, the other is the Questionnaire module (not reviewed here). Both modules are popular, in fact the Questionnaire module has been downloaded more times. The Questionnaire module is based on an open source PHP library for creating surveys called phpESP and offers a lot of flexible question types. The Feedback module is designed specifically for Moodle and is focused on the task of teaching. (Acknowledgement to Randy Orwin for his experience on this.)

## Getting ready

There are two parts to this module: an activity module and a block. The block, when it works, provides links to feedback activities, but this functionality is redundant due to the fact that such links already appear on the central section and in the **Activities** list. Copy the mod/ feedback/ directory from the zip file to the /moodle/mod/ directory. After copying, visit the **Notifications** page and the activity module should be installed.

Once installed, you will be presented with the module's global settings. There is a global setting that, if changed, will allow students to provide feedback that is not associated with their identity at all (total anonymity). If you wish to prevent students from providing feedback as multiple persons, you will want to leave this setting as it is. There is still a level of anonymity with this setting off, however. The system maintains the identity of the Feedback survey participant, but does not provide this in the results. This is the normal level of anonymity and is the recommended default. Even if you make no change, save the settings, or you will be asked to do so each time you return to the **Notifications** page in future.

## How to do it...

When installed, start by creating a Feedback activity. You can create one by selecting **Feedback** from the **Add an activity...** menu. Before you can start creating survey questions, you must set the configuration settings for the Feedback survey.

The configuration begins with typical name and description settings. The name is used as the link text for the activity. The description appears before the survey is started. Keep in mind that there is also a chance later to add text that will appear after the survey has been completed.

Below these **General** settings are some settings specific to the instance of the Feedback activity:

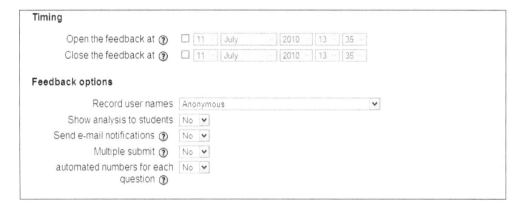

The **Timing** settings allow the teacher to specify a time period during which the Feedback survey is open.

Under **Feedback options**, the first setting controls whether or not student names are collected with their responses. If you are collecting data for research, you will likely want to keep the survey anonymous for ethical reasons. Students are informed about whether the Feedback survey is anonymous or not, and they may be more likely to provide answers (and perhaps more honest answers) if the survey is anonymous.

You can choose to show the analysis of results to students after they complete the Feedback survey or when they return to the activity later. This is achieved by changing the second setting to **Yes**. Consider that showing the results to early submitters may present an unclear picture of what the final results will be like. You might want to set this initially to **No** then allow viewing later in the survey, or after the Feedback survey is closed. If students are able to view the results and then resubmit, this may bias their subsequent responses.

If a teacher wishes to remain informed of when students complete a Feedback survey they can set the option labeled **Send e-mail notification** to **Yes**.

Students can be allowed to resubmit their answers (overriding previous responses if the global setting does not require total anonymity).

After a student has completed the Feedback survey, a page is displayed to them. A message can be specified for that page, with a URL for a continue button, if that is needed.

There are the common group and visibility settings at the end of the configuration page.

Once the module configuration is complete and saved, a page showing the Feedback survey is displayed.

 Only teachers can add questions to a Feedback survey, so if you are logged in as an administrator, you will need to either log in as a teacher, or add yourself as a teacher in the course.

To add questions to the Feedback survey, click on the **Edit questions** tab. There are a variety of question types that allow for both open-ended, qualitative questions, and definitive, quantitative questions.

Labels can be inserted to provide information or group questions together. The questions can be broken over multiple pages by adding page-breaks between questions.

The information needed to specify a question differs for each question type. To create a Likert scale question, use the multiple-choice question type and allow only a single response.

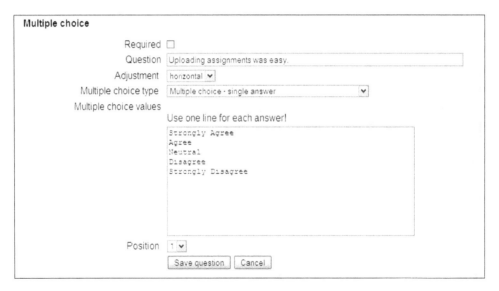

As questions are added, a preview is created.

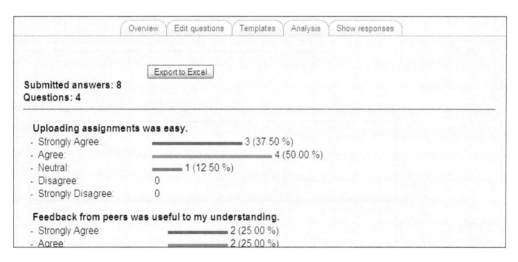

When the questions are finalized, students can begin responding. As they do, their individual responses and an overall analysis of responses are available from the **Show responses** and **Analysis** tabs respectively. The **Analysis** tab is particularly informative:

Responses to multiple-choice questions are presented in chart form. Text responses are collected together. From this view, responses can be exported as an Excel spreadsheet for further analysis.

## There's more...

As well as asking students about their attitudes towards teaching in a course, the Feedback module can be used to collect all kinds of information from students. Here are some ideas:

- Collecting data for a statistics course so that students are analyzing data that is personally relevant
- Allowing students to have input into the future content of the course
- Allowing students to have input on popular issues outside the class

## See also

- Quick Poll block (see the Moodle **Modules and plugins** database)
- Choice module (standard in Moodle)
- Questionnaire module (see the Moodle **Modules and plugins** database)

# 8
# Encouraging Student Interaction

In this chapter, we will cover:

- ▶ Mindmapping
- ▶ Social bookmarking
- ▶ Quick messaging
- ▶ Drawing students into chats, forums, and blogs

## Introduction

In this chapter, we will explore modules that you can use to draw students into shared activities, in order to promote communities of learning within a course.

### Mindmapping

Mindmaps are a great tool for collecting together the thoughts of a group of people. Creating and sharing mindmaps is the purpose of one contributed activity module.

- ▶ Mindmap module

## Social bookmarking

The web is a great source of useful (and sometimes not so useful) information. It can be hard for a teacher to track down a decent collection of web links, so why not ask students to do this and make this part of their learning.

▶ Social Bookmarking module

## Quick messaging

Moodle provides a chat facility, but it is removed from the general context of the course page. There is one block that allows users to write quick messages without leaving the course page.

▶ Shoutbox block

## Drawing students into chats, forums, and blogs

The chat, forum, and blog facilities of Moodle are well designed and very useful for teaching. Students can be asked to use these facilities as part of formative or summative tasks, but creating an atmosphere where students *want* to communicate using these tools, can encourage far greater participation, and openness in a course. There are a few blocks that can be used to draw students into these communication activities.

▶ Chat Users block

▶ Active Forums block

▶ Latest Blog Entries block

# Sharing mindmaps

| | |
|---|---|
| **Name** | Mindmap |
| **Module type** | Activity Module |
| **Author** | ekpenso.com |
| **Released** | 2008 |
| **Maintained** | Limited activity |
| **Languages** | English |
| **Compliance** | Good |
| **Documentation** | Limited |
| **Errors** | None displayed |

Mindmaps were developed by Tony Buzan in the 1970s, as a means of recording thoughts in a non-linear organizational form. A mindmap is a representation of information, organized in a way that is meaningful to the author of the mindmap. A mindmap is presented around a central concept with associated concepts linked to it. Mindmaps can be used as a visual instrument to demonstrate how concepts are associated, or it can be used as a brainstorming tool to collect together the understanding of a cohort around a central topic.

The Mindmap activity module uses a Flash-based mindmapping tool that allows teachers to create mindmaps and also allows students to contribute and collaborate.

## Getting ready

Unzip and copy the `mindmap` directory into the `/moodle/mod/` directory then visit the **Notifications** page.

## How to do it...

Once installed, a **Mindmap** can be added from the **Add an activity...** menu, while editing is turned on. You will then be asked to edit the settings for the activity.

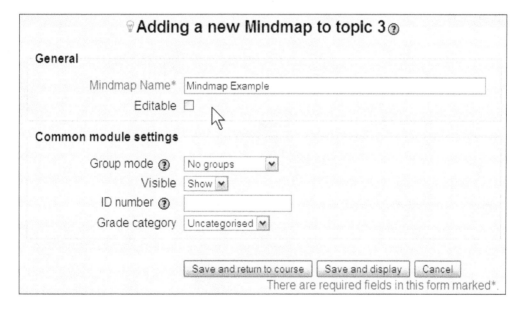

A Mindmap activity must have a name. This name becomes the link text to the activity from the course page.

Unfortunately, there is no potential to add a description to the Mindmap, so if it is being created as an activity for students, task instructions will have to be communicated elsewhere.

There is a second setting, labeled **Editable**, that controls who can edit the mindmap. When checked, students can edit the mindmap. This would be appropriate if the Mindmap activity is being set up for students to complete. If the teacher merely wishes to express concepts related to a course diagrammatically and not allow student editing, this checkbox should be left unchecked.

There was a problem with the version of the Mindmap module reviewed for this book. When a Mindmap activity is created, the **Editable** setting can be checked, allowing all users to edit the mindmap. However, once set, the **Editable** setting cannot be unset. A correction for this is described in the *There's more...* section of the recipe.

In the **Common module settings** there is a setting labeled **Group mode**; however, the Mindmap activity does not allow students to work on mindmaps in groups. Nor can the activity be used as an assessable item.

After the configuration for the activity is set, the mindmap can then be edited.

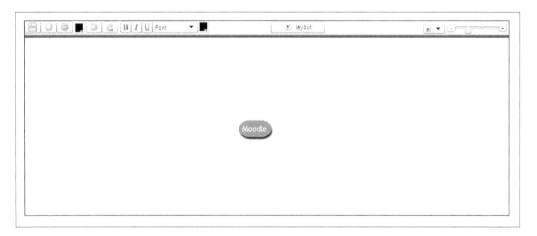

Initially the mindmap text appears quite small. You can zoom in and out on the mindmap using the slider control on the top-right of the mindmap window. Zooming affects the current view only; when the mindmap is reloaded, the default zoom level is used.

The text inside a node of the mindmap can be edited by clicking inside a node. You will then be given the potential to type and alter the node text. Be aware that the focus of text editing will stay with that node until you shift it to another (even after creating new nodes).

To add a node, click the plus icon at the top-left of the mindmap window. Alternately you can press the *Enter* key.

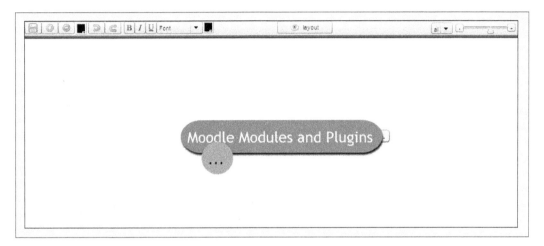

To remove a node, click on it then click the minus icon. Alternately, you can press the *Delete* key after selecting a node. Holding the *Ctrl* key while clicking also deletes a clicked node.

Nodes can be moved by clicking and dragging them. A line should appear between linked nodes to show their relationship.

If the mindmap begins to grow off to one direction, you can move the mindmap within its window by clicking in an empty part of mindmap window and dragging the mindmap. Like the zoom, such shifting only affects the current view as the mindmap re-centres itself around the central concept node when it is reloaded.

Within a mindmap, nodes can have parent-child relationships. An existing node can be made a child of another node by dragging the first onto the second. To add a new node as a child node, select the parent node and press the *Insert* key.

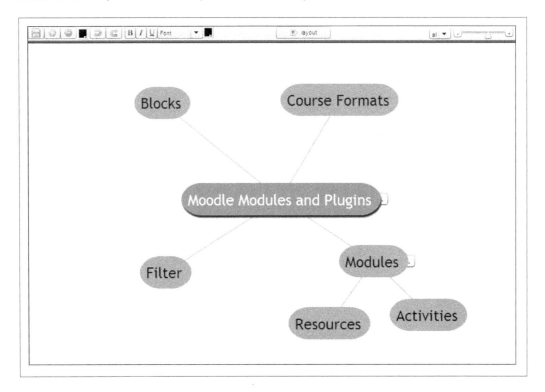

On the toolbar at the top of the mindmap window, there are some controls for fonts and colors. Clicking the **layout** button in the centre of the toolbar causes the nodes to be rearranged into an even and symmetrical layout around the central node.

Once you have added the nodes and organized the relationships you wish to express, click on the save icon (which appears with a floppy disc icon). The module uses Ajax to save the current state of the mindmap in the background.

Ajax combines JavaScript and XML, usually through a library of functions, to create user interfaces in a web browser that can communicate with a web server in the background. Ajax allows the web browser to become an environment for client-side applications which can store and access information to and from a server.

## How it works...

With the **Editable** setting turned off students do not have editing control.

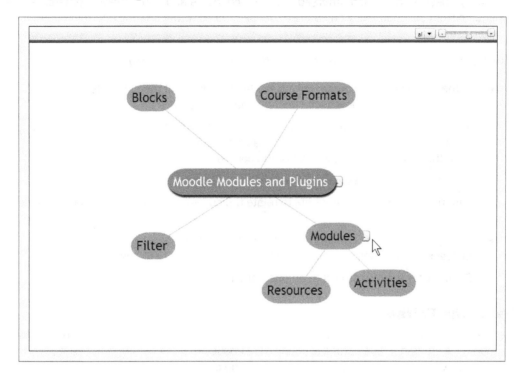

In earlier browsers, such as Internet Explorer 6, functionality is limited. In such browsers there is no capacity to zoom or move the mindmap. Nodes can still be added and moved, however.

Parent nodes appear with a button on their right-hand side. Child nodes can be hidden by clicking this button. Another way of simplifying the mindmap is to show child nodes up to a certain level. There is a control for this next to the zoom slider on the right of the mindmap toolbar. Hiding child nodes does not have a lasting effect on the mindmap, even when the mindmap is saved after hiding nodes.

## There's more...

Of course the real potential of a mindmap is only realized when it is used to bring together the ideas of the collective mind. For this reason, the Mindmap module is an excellent tool for "encouraging student interaction", as the title of this chapter suggests.

According to Benjamin Bloom's *Taxonomy of Educational Objectives*, commonly referred to as *Bloom's Taxonomy*, the exercise of synthesizing separate ideas into a new pattern of thought is a higher level cognitive task. Being asked to contribute to the creation of a mindmap can promote synthesis and cause learners to reflect on concepts and relate them to others. Asking students to work collaboratively on such an exercise will allow the sharing and reinforcement of understandings.

Here are some ideas for how teachers could employ mindmaps in a course:

- At the beginning of a course, asking students to map out the concepts they will cover and anticipate how such concepts may be related
- At the end of a course, asking students to reflect on concepts covered in a course, organizing them in a way they now find appropriate (and how this might differ from what they anticipated at the start of the course)
- Refreshing concepts students have previously learned, after a break
- Within a course, asking students to relate the current topic to related topics outside of the course
- Asking students to relate topical persons to others in the world, either through biological relationships or through related contributions to the world
- Planning for a group project in an open and creative way

## Fixing the Editable setting

There is an **Editable** setting attached to a checkbox on the module's configuration page. After the module is created, if this setting is changed to unchecked, the setting is not saved. This flaw can be overcomed by a simple modification to the code.

Inside the module's folder, locate the `lib.php` file. Using a text editor open this file. Within this file there is a function called `mindmap_update_instance()`, search for this by name. At the end of the function there is a line that begins with the word `return`. Add the following line before the `return` statement near the end of the function.

```
$mindmap->editable = isset($mindmap->editable)?'1':'0';
```

# Encouraging social bookmarking

| Name | Social Bookmarking |
| --- | --- |
| **Module type** | Activity Module |
| **Author** | Ludo (Marc Alier), Jordi Piguillem |
| **Released** | 2008 |
| **Maintained** | Limited |

| Languages | English |
|---|---|
| **Compliance** | Good |
| **Documentation** | Limited |
| **Errors** | None displayed |

Social bookmarking is a practice that allows web users to share sites and pages they are interested in. The key to a successful collection of bookmarks is the set of tags that users define when they bookmark a site. A collection of tags can then be presented to entice users to particular sites. Users can also search using tags.

There are a number of services on the World Wide Web that facilitate general social bookmarking. The Social Bookmarking activity module brings such functionality to a Moodle course.

## Getting ready

You will have to download the module code from the author's website. The `zip` file contains a directory structure with the module code one level deep. Unzip the `/mod/bookmarks/` directory from inside the `zip` file into the `/moodle/mod/` directory and check that the module code now appears in the `/moodle/mod/bookmarks/` directory.

With the module code in place, visit the **Notifications** page to install the module.

## How to do it...

Once installed, you can add a **Bookmarks** activity from the **Add an activity...** menu. The settings for the module include a **Name** and **Description**. The **Name** field will become the text of a link to the activity. The description is a good place to define what bookmarks are to be collected in relation to this activity.

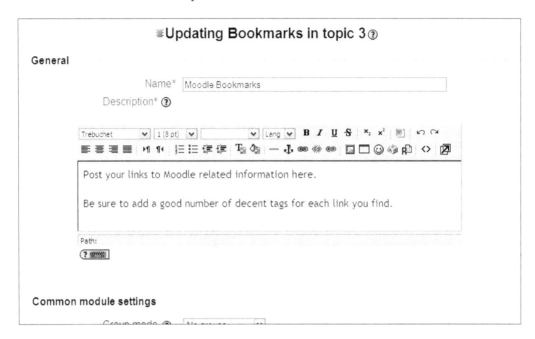

A new Bookmarks activity should appear as follows.

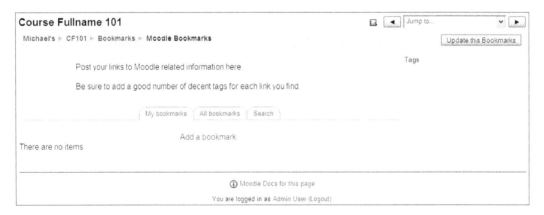

If your view does not appear as the preceding view (with allowances for themes) with the **Tags** area appearing on the right, try refreshing the page while bypassing your browser's cache (_Shift+F5_ should achieve this). Moodle attempts to consolidate all style information for efficiency and may not force your browser to update style information for several days, even if it has changed after the introduction of a new module. This is not a problem for new visitors to a site, or visitors who have not been to the site recently.

As you and your students add bookmarks, they appear in a list, and tags are collected together in the block-like **Tags** area in the form of a tag cloud. Tags are weighted in size according to how often each tag has been used. Clicking on a tag launches a search for bookmarks that use that tag.

Users can see their own bookmarks and those contributed by other users of the activity.

Post your links to Moodle related information here.

Be sure to add a good number of decent tags for each link you find.

My bookmarks    All bookmarks    Search

**Tags**

development xref community download bugs information Moodle LMS code modules documentation reference

**Developer Documentation**
This site shows information for Moodle developers
Tags: lms development documentation
Saved by 1(1) person ... Seen 4 times

**Moodle main website**
The main website for everything Moodle
Tags: moodle
Save... ...mes

**Moc**
This i ...dules for Moodle
Tag:
Sav ...mes

**Moc...** POWERED BY WEBSNAPR.COM

**Mod... ...**
This is the place where you can report bugs and suggest improvements for Moodle related code
Tags: moodle bugs
Saved by 1(1) person ... Seen 0 times

**Moodle.org**
This is the site you will want to go to to find out about Moodle.

Moving the mouse over a link opens a thumbnail preview image of the site. The thumbnail is captured automatically by an external service, so a link to the greater Internet (outside your Moodle site) is required; it is a reasonable assumption that students will have such access seeing that they are bookmarking web links.

The module counts how many times each bookmark is used. This could be motivating for students who see that others are following the bookmarks they have contributed.

Users can search for terms in bookmark descriptions.

The Bookmarks module makes use of the tagging facilities that are already available in Moodle. This means that tags associate with all Bookmark activities in a course can be collected together in a **Tags** block on the course page.

To add a **Tags** block, **Turn editing on** then select the **Tags** block from the **Blocks** menu.

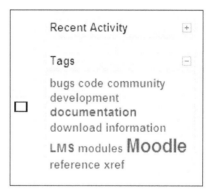

This is a handy way for students to see what tags are becoming popular in the course. Students can associate tags with their profile to define their interests. Unfortunately tags on the **Tags** block do not lead students to bookmarks defined in a Bookmark activity.

## How it works...

In line with modern social networking ideals, the Bookmarks module treats all users as equals, regardless of their role in a course. This simplifies the functionality of the module but also opens up the potential for the module to be abused.

With no teacher moderation there is no way to censor or remove inappropriate bookmarks or descriptions.

## There's more...

Here are some ideas for how to apply social bookmarking in a course:

- ▸ Asking students to search for and bookmark sites relating to the course as a whole
- ▸ Asking students to focus on a single topic and bookmark sites specific to that topic
- ▸ Begin a list of reference materials and standards available on the greater web and ask students to contribute similar links they may find, in order to benefit the entire class
- ▸ Ask students to bookmark topical news items
- ▸ Begin a competition to see who can create bookmarks that are visited by the most students (this will help you discover what really catches students' attention)
- ▸ Open up the module to allow students to experience true social bookmarking

# Getting students to shout

| | |
|---|---|
| **Name** | Shoutbox block |
| **Module type** | Block |
| **Author** | Anil Sharma |
| **Released** | 2009 |
| **Maintained** | Actively |
| **Languages** | English |
| **Compliance** | Poor |
| **Documentation** | None |
| **Errors** | Errors displayed with error reporting enabled |

Chatting can be a useful form of communication in a course. The Chat module takes such simple messaging outside the context of the main course page. The Shoutbox block does not conform to all Moodle conventions; however it is a very simple way to allow students to post quick messages to the whole class, and they can do it right on the course page.

## Getting ready

Unzip and copy the `shoutbox` directory into the `/moodle/blocks/` directory then visit the **Notifications** page.

## How to do it...

Once you have installed the block it can be added by selecting **Shoutbox** from the **Blocks** menu.

### Configuring a Shoutbox block

| | |
|---:|:---|
| Block Title: | Have your say... |
| Number of messages to show: | 4 |
| No. of chars to allow: | 140 |
| No. of chars per line in textbox: | 33 |
| No. of millisecs to refresh: | 1000 |
| Background color of Line 1: | #FFFFFF |
| Background color of Line 2: | #FFFFFF |

Save changes

The default settings need to be altered when the block is added. The default title should reflect what messages you want students to write in the block.

You can set the number of messages shown within the block. This will be determined by what sort of screen real estate you wish to dedicate to this block.

The default maximum message length is five characters, which is probably too short to say anything meaningful. The maximum length of a Twitter tweet is 140 characters, and that is probably a good length here too.

The number of characters in a textbox line defines the width of the input textbox and ultimately the width of the block. You might want to change this if your theme promotes larger or smaller characters.

The final two settings allow the colors of alternating messages to have different backgrounds. These color values are specified in hexadecimal red-green-blue codes. The default is `#FFFFFF` which is white.

When you have saved the configuration settings the block should appear on your course page. If you are using the Ajax course page editing functionality, you may have to **Turn editing off** before you can test the block. As messages are added, they are sent to the database without reloading the page. The block updates to find new messages once in a second (by default) and messages appear within the block without reloading the page.

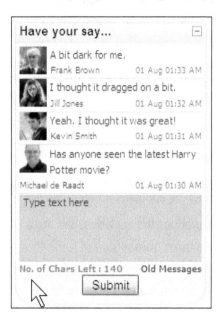

At the bottom of the block there is a link labeled **Old messages**. Clicking this link pops up a browser window with a history of messages. Students can edit their own messages in this view. Teachers and administrators can edit and delete all messages. There is also potential to download a list of messages, which can be useful as a way of assessing students, or perhaps can be used as research data.

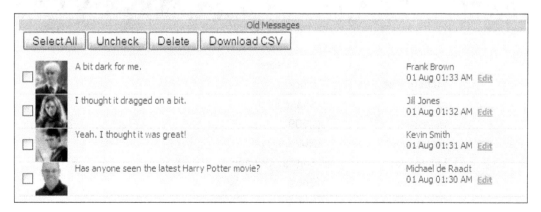

## How it works...

The block uses Ajax, which in basic terms means small requests for information from the server. Where a normal web page request will deliver an entire page, an Ajax request can deliver a small piece of structured information which can be used to replace the content of a part of a page.

 In previous versions of the Shoutbox block there have been incompatibilities with some versions of Internet Explorer. The author claims these problems have been resolved, but you will want to get the latest version of Shoutbox.

## There's more...

The Shoutbox block is perhaps best used for casual communication and social discussion, but it can be applied to real teaching applications. Here are some ideas:

▸ Allowing students to introduce themselves to the class

▸ Testing students with a quick question

▸ Asking students for real world examples related to a current topic

▸ Answering questions received during a scheduled online session

## See also

▸ Chat activity module (standard in Moodle)

▸ Chat Users block

# Promoting chatter

| | |
|---|---|
| **Name** | Chat Users |
| **Module type** | Block |
| **Author** | Shane Elliott |
| **Released** | 2009 |
| **Maintained** | Not really |
| **Languages** | English, German |
| **Compliance** | Good |
| **Documentation** | None |
| **Errors** | None displayed |

The Chat activity module allows students and teachers to communicate synchronously. However synchronous communication is predicated by users knowing that there is someone online to chat to in the first place. The Chat Users block shows that users are currently chatting and invites others to join them.

## Getting ready

Unzip and copy the block directory into `/moodle/blocks/` then visit the **Notifications** page.

## How to do it...

A Chat Users block needs to be associated with a Chat activity, so before adding this block you will first want to create a Chat activity. Choose **Chat** from the **Add an activity...** menu and complete the settings for the activity.

Add a **Chat Users** block from the **Blocks** menu. After it is added you will need to configure the block.

The Chat Users block will show a list of users in a single Chat activity. You will need to choose which Chat activity; the block will not assume anything (even if you only have a single Chat activity in a course). This could be useful if you have multiple Chat activities and want to show separate lists of users for each.

You will want to add a **Block title** as the default block title **New Chat Users Block** assumes it will be overridden. If you have multiple Chat activities and are adding a Chat Users block for each, this is a chance to distinguish which Chat activity the block is monitoring.

## How it works...

While there are no users in the Chat activity, the block makes this explicit, but still allows users to enter the Chat activity.

When users are chatting, their profile pictures and names appear in the block's list. Clicking on a user's name displays a user profile page.

The Chat Users block shows users who are chatting at the time when page is loaded. The block doesn't update dynamically, so if a user hasn't reloaded the course page for some time before they enter a Chat activity, they may be disappointed to discover that the list of chatting users has become outdated.

Clicking the link labeled **Enter chat** pops up a chat window without reloading the course page, which is quite convenient, although it assumes users will use the JavaScript version of the Chat activity.

# Finding active forums

| | |
|---|---|
| **Name** | Active Forums |
| **Module type** | Block |
| **Author** | Siau Meng Nyam |
| **Released** | 2010 |
| **Maintained** | Actively (it's quite new) |
| **Languages** | English, Hebrew |
| **Compliance** | Good |
| **Documentation** | Help files |
| **Errors** | None displayed |

Forums are the staple form of asynchronous communication in Moodle. Discussion forums in general have been proven to have benefits for learners; however, one of the difficulties in using forums is luring students to participate.

The Active Forums block shows discussion activity in the form of a tag cloud. The titles of discussions that are more active appear larger and bolder; less active forums appear diminutively. The intention is to involve students in conversations that are currently active in the course.

## Getting ready

Unzip and copy the `active_forums` directory into the `/moodle/blocks/` directory then visit the **Notifications** page.

## How to do it...

Once installed, you can leave the default settings and let the block inform students of active discussions. It is possible to configure the block if you have specific intentions.

### Configuring a Active Forums block

| | |
|---:|:---|
| Block instance title: ⑦ | Active Forums |
| Period checked (days): ⑦ | 7 ▾ |
| Maximum name length before truncation: ⑦ | 20 ▾ |
| Maximum discussions in tag cloud: ⑦ | 10 ▾ |
| Include News forums: ⑦ | No ▾ |

Save changes

It is possible to re-title the block. The purpose of this is to allow multiple instances of the block that may each cover different periods of time, for example, one that shows the most active discussions in the last seven days and another that shows the most active forums over the entire course. You could also re-title the block with something more meaningful, especially if there is not a translation available in your native language.

The block looks for posts over the last seven days, by default. This period can be extended up to 180 days.

As discussion titles can be quite long, and as block space is limited, lengthy titles are truncated. The maximum length before a title is truncated can be controlled. Similarly, the number of displayed discussions can be controlled. By default, the top 10 active discussions are shown.

In Moodle, the Forum activity module is used for two purposes. News forums are used to make announcements and don't involve students. General forums are used for student interaction. News forums are not included among active discussions displayed in the block, unless the default for the final **Include News forums** setting is changed.

## How it works...

The forum looks for activity in discussions within the course. It orders them by the count of recent posts and forms the result into a weighted tag cloud.

Clicking on a discussion title takes the user directly to the active discussion.

## See also

▶   Unanswered Discussions block (see **Modules and plugins** database)

# Encouraging blogging

| Name | Latest Blog Entries |
|------|---------------------|
| **Module type** | Block |
| **Author** | Ludo (Marc Alier), Fernando Oliveira |
| **Released** | 2006 |
| **Maintained** | Limited |
| **Languages** | English |
| **Compliance** | Good |
| **Documentation** | None available |
| **Errors** | None displayed |

Blogs are a great way of encouraging students to reflect on their learning. Personal blogs in a Moodle site can be shared and read by other users, regardless of course. One of the main reasons people write blog entries is so that their words can be read by others. However, apart from viewing personal blogs through users' profiles, there is not a simple way of announcing user's blog entries on course pages.

The Latest Blog Entries block promotes the blogs of course participants by advertising their latest postings. This block seems to have been abandoned by the original author, but another developer has released an updated version of the block which you will find attached to the original **Modules and plugins** database entry for this block. This review is based on that updated version.

## Getting ready

Unzip and copy the `fn_updated_blogs` directory into the `/moodle/blocks/` directory then visit the **Notifications** page.

## How to do it...

When first added, you will be asked to set values for global settings associated with the block.

**New settings - FN Updated Blogs**

| | | |
| --- | --- | --- |
| Maximum number of blogs to show | 10 | Default: Empty |
| block_updated_blogs_viewmax | Maximum number of blogs to show | |
| Layout of the list | Rows ☑ | Default: Rows |
| block_updated_blogs_layout | Layout of the list | |

The first setting controls how many blog entries are advertised in the block. Entries are limited to titles and a few other details, so each blog entry does not take up much space, however, if screen real-estate is tight on your course pages, perhaps a lower maximum may be appropriate.

The second global setting relates to the presentation of blog updates. The original version of this block showed entries as rows in a table with features presented in separate columns. The updated version offers a view with each entry as a single row containing a number of lines rather than columns. This updated view provides a less cramped presentation of entries, so the default **Rows** option is what you will probably want to use.

At the course page, a Latest Blog Entries block can be added by selecting **FN Updated Blogs** from the **Blocks** menu.

When the block is added you will want to edit the single configuration setting.

**Configuring a FN Updated Blogs block**

Display title: Recently Updated Blogs

Save changes

This setting allows you to use a more meaningful title compared to **FN Updated Blogs**. For a remedy to change the default setting globally, see the *There's more...* section of this recipe.

The block will show recent blog entries, grouped together by date.

Ultimately the purpose of using this block is to draw students into the blogs of other users, and hopefully promote the use of blogs by all users. A second block that you might, therefore, want to add alongside the Latest Blogs Entries block (preceding screenshot) is the standard **Blog Menu** block. This block allows users to quickly access their own blog and begin writing.

## There's more...

Blogs are a great example of social computing. They are an easy-to-use tool, allowing students and teachers to report their thoughts and experiences. Reflection is a higher-level cognitive task, so encouraging reflection allows users to have a deeper learning experience and become more aware of what they do and don't understand.

Blogs also provide the potential for students to build on the knowledge of their peers. This engenders a community of learning, allowing learners to feel less isolated in their studies, regardless of whether they are located close by or separated by great distances.

Blogs allow students to develop public writing skills, which are becoming far more valuable as electronically mediated communication becomes a greater part of our lives.

## Changing the block name in Blocks list

The updated version of the Latest Blog Entries block uses the title **FN Updated Blogs** in the **Blocks** list and as a default title for new instances of the block. This title might not be meaningful to teaching.

There are two ways to change this title. The first is to edit the `block_fn_updated_blogs.php` file located in `/moodle/blocks/fn_updated_blogs/lang/en_utf8/` directory.

The other way to make minor changes to a module's language strings is by using Moodle's **Language editing** tool. While logged in as an administrator, navigate to your site's root page. In the **Site Administration** menu, expand the **Language** item and click on **Language editing**. You will be asked to choose a language from the languages installed in the system. Assuming you choose **English(en)** you will be able to edit English language files. This tool is also useful for creating translations for other languages, although perhaps not as convenient as editing the language files themselves. With your language selected, click on the link titled **Edit words or phrases**. You will be presented with a drop-down list of installed modules. Contributed modules are listed at the bottom of this list. Locate the **block_fn_updated_blogs** entry.

Make changes to the two strings labeled **FN Updated Blogs** and save changes using the button at the bottom of the page.

# 9
# Informing Students

In this chapter, we will cover:

- ▶ Locating online students
- ▶ Rating courses
- ▶ Simplifying announcements
- ▶ Timely information

## Introduction

This chapter reveals a number of blocks that can be useful in communicating general information to students. This kind of information is not related to materials or assessment, but is still important for students.

### Locating online students

Moodle is an excellent learning management system for courses that cater to students studying at a distance. But students studying remotely can feel isolated.

Being able to see that other students are online is a great motivator. Creating a sense of community allows students to feel that they are not alone in their studies. Seeing where online users are located around the world can add an element of significance to the community studying a course.

We will look at a block that complements the Online Users block, to show online users located in a small Google map:

- Online Users Google Map block

## Rating courses

Asking for feedback from students can be like pulling teeth. This invaluable information is very hard to extract from students. Simplifying the task of providing feedback to a simple rating out of five stars might not be appropriate for all courses, but it is certainly simpler and may encourage more students to provide feedback. It also provides a quick, visual aid for comparing courses:

- Rate a course block

## Simplifying announcements

Announcements from teachers to students are an important part of any course. We look at a block that improves on the standard Latest News block to provide relevant information in more compact form:

- FN – Announcements block

## Timely information

Time plays a part in all learning. But how much time? We will look at a number of blocks that allow teachers to make time a more explicit part of their course:

- Countdown block
- Analog Clock block
- Simple Clock block

# Geolocating students

| Name | Online Users Google Map |
|---|---|
| **Module type** | Block |
| **Author** | Alex Little |
| **Released** | 2007 |
| **Maintained** | Actively |
| **Languages** | English, French, German, Hungarian, Portugese, Spanish |
| **Compliance** | Good |
| **Documentation** | `Readme.txt` file |
| **Errors** | None displayed |

Using a learning management system for teaching means that students can access material and participate in activities at all hours of the day. The Online Users block is a standard block in Moodle, and shows users who are online (or have been online very recently). It is often amazing to log on to a course website late at night and find that there are still a number of users working away in a course.

The Online Users Google Map block shows participants who are online, not by name, but by location. Now students can see that they are not alone in their studies, and that the students in the course come from all over the map.

## Getting ready

Unzip and copy the `online_users_map` block directory into the `/moodle/blocks/` directory then visit the **Notifications** page.

 This module requires access to information from outside your site. The cURL library needs to be enabled in your PHP settings. See *Chapter 1, Getting Modular with Moodle* for information on enabling cURL.

## How to do it...

After the block is installed, you will be taken to the global settings page for the block:

**New settings - Online Users Map**

| | | |
|---|---|---|
| Remove after inactivity | 5 | Default: 5 |
| block_online_users_map_timetosee | | Number of minutes determining the period of inactivity after which a user is no longer considered to be online. |
| Google Maps API key | | Default: Empty |
| block_online_users_map_google_api_key | | Google Maps API key, obtain a key from http://code.google.com /apis/maps/signup.html |
| Initial latitude | 0 | Default: 0 |
| block_online_users_map_centre_lat | | Initial central latitude of the map - in plain decimal format (not degrees/minutes) |

There is one particular setting that needs attention, and that is the **Google Maps API key**. If you already have an API key for the Map module (reviewed in *Chapter 2, Effective Use of Space*), then you can reuse that key. If you don't already have one, you can obtain a key from the link provided below the **Google Maps API key** setting. Clicking this link launches a new window and takes you to the Google Maps API site.

Enter the URL of your site. If you are running a test server, it is OK to enter `http://localhost`. You will need to agree to Google's terms and conditions then press the button labeled **Generate API Key**.

When a key is generated it is presented in a number of formats. The value you need is the first string of letters and numbers.

**Sign Up for the Google Maps API**

**Thank You for Signing Up for a Google Maps API Key!**

Your key is:

`ABQIAAAAXp2mBuE7thnybwwPq82e7xT2yXp_ZAY8_ufC3CFXhHIE1NvwkxS08vawHbxXNm9vCyzBTzsSihk_zw`

Paste this value back into the global settings page for the Online Users Google Map and save these settings.

Another setting you might consider changing is the initial zoom value. If all your students come from one country or a smaller area, you might consider increasing the zoom level to a value greater than zero, to focus on where students are located. Users can zoom in and out manually once the block is loaded. Users are differentiated by what town they are located in, so there is no distinction between users located in a single town.

Once installed, you can add an **Online Users Map** block by selecting this option from the **Blocks** menu. There are no instance settings for this block.

## How it works...

The Online Users Google Map block shows the location of users in the current course, centered around the user's own location. Users who are online (or have been in the last five minutes) are shown with green markers.

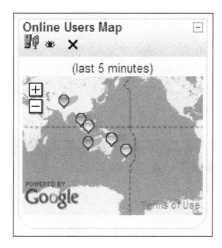

It is possible to zoom in and out on the map, right down to the local level. The map can also be dragged to re-centre it. Moving the mouse over a marker reveals the name of the user it represents.

## There's more...

In Moodle, the location of each user is identified by a town and a country. Before these locations can be displayed on a map, the longitude and latitude values for these locations need to be discovered. It takes a second or so to translate the map location for each town, so it would be very inefficient to undertake this each time the block loads. Instead, the block creates a Cron job to translate and cache locations of users in the background. If you add the block to a course page before such a search takes place, you will see an empty map. If you are running a test server, you might not have a Cron program running at all. To force the Cron script to run, direct your browser to the following URL `http://localhost/moodle/admin/cron.php`. If you are running Moodle on a real server, replace `localhost` with the hostname of your server.

Cron is the name of a program that runs on a server and performs tasks in the background on a regular basis. A number of Moodle modules make use of the Cron process to update settings. An example is the Forum module, which on a regular basis, needs to send e-mails about new posts to users. For more information about the use of Cron in Moodle, visit `http://docs.moodle.org/en/Cron`.

## See also

▸ Map module (see *Chapter 2, Adding Content*)

# Gauging course quality

| Name | Rate a course |
| --- | --- |
| **Module type** | Block |
| **Author** | Jenny Gray |
| **Released** | 2009 |
| **Maintained** | Actively |
| **Languages** | English, German |
| **Compliance** | Exemplary |
| **Documentation** | Online documentation |
| **Errors** | None displayed |

Feedback on a course informs both teachers and students about the perceived quality of a course. For students, such information can assure them of the quality of education they are receiving. For teachers, feedback is essential to improve their teaching efforts.

Feedback can be as complex as an in-depth survey. The Feedback module reviewed earlier in this book is an excellent tool for such information gathering. A quick poll using the choice activity can also be a course-quality feedback mechanism.

The amount of feedback received from students can be affected by the effort required to provide feedback. Asking for a quick rating, such as a rating out of five stars, is simple and can entice more users to provide feedback. Certainly this method is popular on commercial websites to request consumer feedback.

Not all Moodle instances are used in regular classroom situations. Often Moodle is used in an open manner, allowing students to enroll in courses based on their interests. In such cases, providing a simple rating for each course could potentially lure students into a course they might otherwise have avoided.

The Rate a course block provides a simple way for students to give feedback, and also allows such course ratings to be used in flexible ways.

## Getting ready

Unzip and copy the `rate_course` directory into the `/moodle/blocks/` directory, then visit the **Notifications** page.

## How to do it...

Once installed, you can add a **Course ratings** block from the **Blocks** menu.

There are no settings associated with the block. It's really quite simple—add it and it works.

## How it works...

Once added the block appears as follows.

Users can see the current rating and add their own rating by clicking the link labeled **Give a rating**.

To give a rating, a new page opens and the following simple form is shown to the user:

Users can choose a numeric rating from 1 to 5. The levels are not defined, so the responses received from users will be based purely on their implied notion of quality, perhaps influenced by varied experiences they may have had.

By default, there is no distinction between the roles of users who can give feedback. It is open to students, teachers, course creators, and administrators. When the block is installed, a permission item is created, so it is possible to remove rating permission by role. Role permissions can be changed at a site or course level. If you wanted to disallow teachers from rating their own courses, you can affect the setting at **Site Administration | Users | Permissions | Define roles**; click on the **Teacher** role; then click on **Edit**, then change the permission labeled **Give a rating to a course** to **Prevent**.

An identity must be linked to each rating, so users cannot give a rating while they are not logged in or if they are logged in as a guest.

Users cannot change their rating. If they attempt to give a rating a second time, they are presented with the following screen:

As users provide their ratings, the current course rating is presented each time the block is reloaded:

The stars appear fully opaque or partially transparent. Each star can be a full star or a half star. The overall average rating is therefore rounded to the nearest half star, leaving 10 possible displays. Each display of stars is represented by a PNG image. Unfortunately the PNG transparency doesn't work in IE6 as it does in other browsers, but the message is still reasonably clear.

There is no way to reset ratings for a course. Even when block is deleted the ratings are retained in the database, so if the block is re-added it will include previous ratings.

## There's more...

The block is an excellent way to collect a rating for a course. Once collected, a rating can be accessed from elsewhere in the course or around the site.

One suggestion for a rating display is within the course list on site root page. To achieve this you need to be confident enough to modify Moodle core code. If you are game, open the following file in your editor.

```
/moodle/course/lib.php
```

Within this file, locate the `print_course()` function, this function outputs a row of the course list table, relating to a single course. Towards the end of the function there are two `echo` statements used to output two `</div>` tags. Add the following lines of code immediately before those two `echo` statements:

```
echo '<div style="font-size:small;text-align:center;color:#666666;">';
$block = block_instance('rate_course');
$block->display_rating($course->id);
echo '</div>';
```

This new code instantiates the `rate_course` block object and calls the `display_rating()` method for a particular course. This will output the appropriate star rating image and number of ratings for the identified course. The output of this change appears as follows:

---

## Available Courses

Lorem Ipsum 101
    Teacher: Frank Brown
    Teacher: Jodie Blyth

Lorem ipsum dolor sit amet, consectetur adipiscing elit. Etiam at eros vitae diam aliquam commodo vitae in dolor. Donec id nibh in eros dignissim posuere. In dictum cursus volutpat. In mollis massa et mauris lacinia vitae sollicitudin dui molestie. Nunc vitae ante quis ipsum lobortis ullamcorper molestie sit amet enim.

No ratings given

Course Fullname 101
    Teacher: Michael de Raadt

Rated by 6 user(s)

---

Now students can see the ratings of each course from the list of courses. If they are free to choose a course, they may be more likely to choose a course if it has a high star rating.

You are within your rights to modify core and contributed Moodle code. You should be aware, however, that this comes with some risk. Apart from possible unexpected side effects, once you have changed core code, if you update your instance of Moodle in future, the code will be overwritten and you will need to re-do any changes you previously made.

## See also

> ▸ Feedback module (see *Chapter 7, Organizing Students*)
> ▸ Choice module (standard in Moodle)

# Notifying announcements

| Name | FN - Announcements |
|---|---|
| **Module type** | Block |
| **Author** | Fernando Oliveira, Mike Churchward |
| **Released** | 2009 |
| **Maintained** | Limited |
| **Languages** | English |
| **Compliance** | Good |
| **Documentation** | `Readme.txt` file |
| **Errors** | None displayed |

The Announcements block is an enhancement on the Latest News block. It allows a customizable title, it is more compact and it utilizes forum read tracking.

## Getting ready

Unzip and copy the `fn_announcements` block directory into the `/moodle/blocks/` directory then visit the **Notifications** page.

## How to do it...

Once installed, the block can be added by selecting **FN_Announcements** from the **Blocks** menu.

The block can be used to replace the Latest News forum. They are shown here adjacent to each other for comparison:

Clicking the configuration icon allows a teacher to change the single setting for the block:

Using this setting the teacher can change the block title. The default title used when this setting is empty is "Announcements".

## How it works...

The Announcements block shows the same News forum topics as the Latest News block, but in a more compact form. The date and author information for each message are not included to save on space.

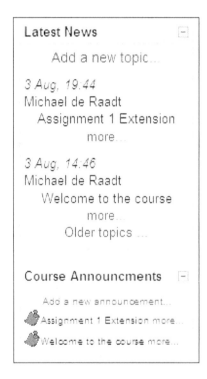

Teachers are provided with a link to add a news forum item. The link does not appear for students.

The icon color can change from red to yellow if the user has read the news forum message, but only if the **Forum Tracking** option is set to **Yes: highlight new posts for me** in the current user's profile. This is an advanced setting and defaults to **No: don't keep track of posts I have read**.

## There's more...

This is a handy little block that helps inform students about news messages they may have missed, but only if forum tracking is turned on for the student. The students themselves can enable tracking, but only if they know about it or they go searching through the advanced profile settings.

### Enabling forum read tracking by default

Forum tracking is a very useful feature, and it is turned off by default for new users. It's actually not a simple matter to change the default for this setting.

If you enter students manually, you can turn tracking on by default by altering the default form value used when creating a new user. Open the file /moodle/users/editlib.php. The default for the trackforums setting is defined at (or around) line **164**. Change the default value from 0 to 1 so that the statement looks as follows.

```
$mform->setDefault('trackforums', 1);
```

If you use the bulk user upload facility, the trackforums field cannot be included as a field in the CVS file you upload, nor can a default value be set using the interface while uploading the file. To change the default for new users you need to change the default value for the trackforums field in the database. Locate the table using your DBMS interface and change the default value for this field from 0 to 1.

# Counting down

| Name | Countdown block |
|---|---|
| Module Type | Block |
| Author | Matthew Cannings |
| Released | 2007 |
| Maintained | Actively |
| Languages | English, Polish (available separately) |
| Compliance | OK |
| Documentation | `Readme.txt` file |
| Errors | Errors displayed when error reporting is turned on |

The Countdown block allows a teacher to build anticipation towards an event or some point in time. The block displays a countdown in a number of simple formats, making use of a Flash animation.

 There is an assumption that students will have the Flash plug-in installed in their browser; while this is quite likely, the block should not be relied upon to convey critical information.

## Getting ready

The block needs to be downloaded from the author's site.

Copy the `countdown` directory from the zip file into the `/moodle/blocks/` directory. There are a number of FLA files at the root of the same `zip` file that do not need to be copied.

Visit the **Notifications** page to install the block.

## How to do it...

Once installed, you will want to adjust the global settings for the block. Navigate to **Site Administration | Modules | Blocks | Countdown**:

## Countdown

Be careful modifying these settings -
strange values could cause problems.

Width  [135]    (Default = 135)

Height  [85]    (Default = 85)

Start Year  [2010]    End Year  [2020]

[ Save changes ]

You will need to adjust the **Start Year** and **End Year** settings to create a range of years that a teacher can select from when configuring the block. The default range from 2008 to 2010 is becoming dated (literally).

With global configuration settings in place, you can now add the block to a course page. The block appears listed as **Countdown** in the **Blocks** list.

After adding the block, click on the configuration icon to change the settings for the block. The block configuration stretches over a number of screens.

### Configuring a Countdown block

Title:  [Countdown to New Year]    (leave blank to hide the title)

Time Source:  ○ Server Time
⊙ User's computer

Clock Style:

days **150**  hrs **02**
mins **10**  secs **36**

**150 days**
**02:10:36**

**12967836**
**Seconds**
**Remain**

ave Countdown:

At the top of the configuration page are settings that control the clock's appearance. First, there is a setting that allows you to set a title for the block. This is a good place to indicate what the Countdown block is counting down to, although there are also settings that allow you to add text before and/or after the countdown clock. Leaving the **Title** setting blank will cause the block header to be hidden (when editing is turned off).

The second setting allows a teacher to choose whether the countdown relies on the **User's computer** or the **Server Time**. Normally using the server clock as a basis for the countdown would be preferable, as this would achieve greater accuracy, consistency, and also ensure students studying remotely are seeing the countdown in the local time zone at the Moodle site. However, during testing, the server time functionality didn't work; instead the countdown ended abruptly when the block was shown. Assuming you are not using the block for any critically important form of countdown (the next rocket launch perhaps), the **User's computer** setting can be used.

The third setting allows you to choose from three clock formats. All formats fit nicely in a block space, so the choice will depend on what you want to emphasize.

Scrolling down on the configuration page reveals more settings.

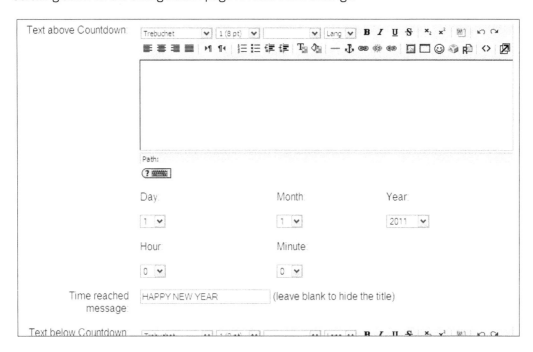

The first advanced text editor allows you to add text that will appear in the block above the countdown. Following this are some settings that are of critical importance to the countdown; they are the date and time to count down to. For the year, there is an **annual** option which causes the clock to begin a new countdown once it reaches its goal, aiming at the same time each year.

Following the time settings there is a textbox that can be used to input a message that will appear when the goal is reached. This needs to be simple text as it is displayed in the Flash element.

Towards the bottom of the configuration page there is a final screen of settings.

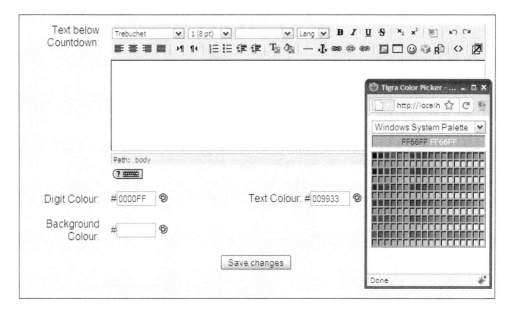

The advanced text editor labeled **Text below Countdown** allows the teacher to specify a message that will appear below the countdown Flash object.

Finally, there are three settings to control the colors of the digits, the text, and the background of the countdown object. The values that need to be entered for these settings use hexadecimal red-green-blue codes. Clicking the palette icon next to each setting pops up a small window that allows the user to select a color; the corresponding code is placed into the appropriate setting.

## How it works...

The countdown appears in the block, in the format specified. The clock updates itself before your eyes:

There is no option to disable the display of seconds, so each second slips by in animated style. This could be distracting for students who may be attempting to concentrate on something in the central area of the page.

## There's more...

Here are some ideas for how the Countdown block could be used in a Moodle course:

- Countdown to an assignment or exam deadline
- Countdown to a topical event related to the course (for example, an election)
- Countdown to the holidays
- Where a Moodle instance is used for a public event, such as a conference, there could be a countdown to the start of the event

## See also

- Simple Clock block
- Analog Clock block

# Keeping time

| Name | Analog Clock Block | Simple Clock |
|------|-------------------|--------------|
| **Module type** | Block | Block |
| **Author** | Amr Hourani | Michael de Raadt |
| **Released** | 2006 | 2010 |
| **Maintained** | Actively | Actively (it's still new) |
| **Languages** | English | English |
| **Compliance** | Good | Good |
| **Documentation** | Limited | Online documentation, help files |
| **Errors** | None displayed | None displayed |

A clock can be a useful tool for students, especially when activities are due at specified times. Here we present two clock blocks that can be used for various purposes.

The Analog Clock block is a simple clock that utilizes a Flash object to show the current time. As well as being an appealing representation of the time, it could also be useful in the classroom for students learning to tell the time from an analog clock.

The Simple Clock block is primarily designed to show the difference in time between the Moodle server and the student's computer. This will help the student to understand when activities with deadlines are due at the server.

 The Analog Clock block requires a Flash plug-in and the Simple Clock block utilizes JavaScript in the user's browser. If you think students will not have these capabilities, you may not be able to rely on these blocks to display the time.

## Getting ready

The Analog Clock block is packaged as a `Rar` file; if you are using Windows or Mac, you may need an alternate compression program to unpack this block.

Unzip and copy the block directories into the `/moodle/blocks/` directory, then visit the **Notifications** page.

Once installed, you can add each of these blocks and they will work nicely without modification. If you wish to customize the blocks, there are some settings you can affect.

The Analog Clock block has global settings that control the size of the clock Flash object used within the block. To access these settings navigate to the site root page, then use the menu to reach **Site Administration | Modules | Blocks | Clock**:

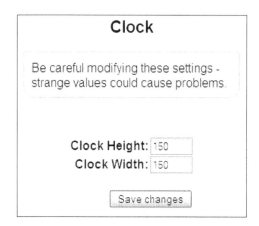

The default settings offer a circular clock that fits into a block column easily. If you are limited for screen real-estate you might consider reducing the size in both dimensions. Alternately, if you have visually impaired students, you may choose to increase the size of the clock. Changes made to these global settings affect the appearance of the block throughout the site.

Once you are satisfied with the global settings for the Analog Clock block, you can add it to a course page by selecting **Clock** from the **Blocks** menu. There are no instance settings for the Analog Clock block.

The Simple Clock block has no global settings, but does have instance settings. First you must add an instance of the block by selecting **Simple Clock** from the **Blocks** menu. Once added you can access the configuration settings by clicking the configuration icon.

## Configuring a Simple Clock block

| | |
|---|---|
| Instance title ⑦ | Clock |
| Visible clocks ⑦ | Show clocks for both server and user ▾ |
| Seconds ⑦ | ☐ Show seconds with each clock |
| Header ⑦ | ☐ Hide the header (effective after turning editing off) |
| Icons ⑦ | ☐ Hide the clock icons |
| | Save changes |

The Simple Clock block offers a number of settings to control the appearance and functionality of the block. A help file is supplied for each setting.

The title of the block can be changed. The default is **Simple Clock**, which you might wish to change to **Clock**. Alternately you might want to indicate that the clock shows the time at your institution, for example **USQ Time**. If you are running a small instance of Moodle and teaching in a language other than English, re-titling the clock in your language is probably simpler than creating a new language file for the block.

By default, two clocks are shown; one for the server and one for the user. You can change this to show a single clock, either for the server or for the user.

In the Simple Clock block, seconds are not shown by default. You can turn seconds on if you wish to show a more precise time. The header of the block can be hidden to reduce space. The site icon is shown next to the server clock and the user's picture is shown next to the user's clock. These icons can be disabled.

## How it works...

The Analog Clock block appears as a simple, elegant clock, with hour, minute, and second hands.

Unfortunately there are no options to change the appearance of the clock face. For use with students in early school years, showing the hour numbers would be ideal.

The animation of the second hand is smooth and continuous. Unfortunately, this caused a measurable increase in CPU usage on the client machine during testing. The increase was ±10% of a 1.6 GHz processor, which was not huge, but was noticeable.

The Simple Clock block will appear formatted according to the configuration settings:

The names of the two clocks are **Server** and **You**. These names are not configurable in the instance settings. If you wish to change the names of the clocks, this can be achieved in the language file located at `/moodle/blocks/simple_clock/lang/en_utf8/block_simple_clock.php`. Alternately you can affect the language strings using the language tool at **Site Administration | Language | Language Editing**.

## There's more...

Apart from the obvious use of these blocks to show the current time, such blocks can be used for educational purposes. Here are some ideas:

- Teaching students to read time in analog and digital formats
- Demonstrating that time can differ by location according to the accuracy of different clocks (including computer clocks)
- Demonstrating the time difference between time zones
- Limiting student "free time" provided as a reward for completing set work

## See also

- Countdown block

# 10
# Handy Tools for Teachers

In this chapter, we will cover:

- ▶ Sharing and cloning activities and resources
- ▶ Quickly searching for users
- ▶ Examining time online
- ▶ Getting user statistics

## Introduction

Teaching can be a rewarding profession, but too often it is monotonous drudgery. Tools that can make a teacher more effective are always welcome.

In this chapter, we reveal a number of blocks designed to improve the lot of humble teachers; the people working at the coal-face, with their nose to the grindstone and their ear to the ground. Yeah—those guys.

## Sharing and cloning activities and resources

From week-to-week and course-to-course, a lot of activities and resources need to be created and many will be quite similar to what has been created before. In Moodle, each new activity and resource has to be created from scratch, and copying the settings and formatting from one item to the next is tedious. But there is a block that facilitates the cloning of activities and resources, between topics and weeks, and across courses:

- Sharing Cart block

## Quickly searching for users

Each student (and user) has a profile in a Moodle system. For students, this is accompanied by information about their activity in the course, which is valuable for teachers needing to make decisions. Reaching a user's profile can require several steps and an amount of searching. Being able to search for users by name or even using partial strings allows a quicker route to profiles:

- Quickfind User List

## Examining time online

Student activity data shows when a user was first online and last online, but not how long they have been online. To gauge how long users are spending online requires a bit of crafty thinking and some nifty database querying. Fortunately there is a block that achieves this:

- Course Dedication block

## Getting user statistics

For sites big and small, it's always valuable to have a picture of the scale of the problem you are up against. There are a number of blocks that can graphically demonstrate the level of user activity and growth, allowing you to properly resource your site and the courses you run:

- Usage block
- User Growth block
- Graph Stats block

# Cloning activities and resources

| Name | Sharing Cart |
|---|---|
| **Module type** | Block |
| **Author** | Akio Ohnishi, Don Hinkelman, Andrew Johnson |
| **Released** | 2009 |
| **Maintained** | Actively |
| **Languages** | English, Japanese, Spanish |
| **Compliance** | Good |
| **Documentation** | Help file, online documentation |
| **Errors** | None displayed |

In Moodle, if you want to create an activity or resource you need to start from scratch. But teaching is often a repetitive business. If you want to create a new item similar to an existing item, typically you have to copy each setting, one-by-one.

The Sharing Cart is a convenient tool for teachers who have been around a while. It allows you to clone activities and resources, even from one course to another. You no longer have to start from scratch. Now you can copy that assignment, alter the description, change the due date, and you're done. Web pages can be copied to preserve formatting between instances. That same old forum that appears with every topic in your course can now be copied once and added multiple times, each in just a few clicks. If you're really prepared, you can even store templates for activities and resources in your Sharing Cart and bring them out as a starting point each time you need one.

With the Sharing Cart you can even copy the activities and resources from other teachers' courses, as long as you have access to their course. Equally, they can copy items from your courses in a simpler way than using the course import function.

## Getting ready

Unzip and copy the `sharing_cart` block directory into the `/moodle/blocks/` directory, then visit the **Notifications** page.

## How to do it...

There is a global settings page for this block. You will be taken to it after visiting the **Notifications** page.

The Sharing Cart block is built to be modular. The global settings page allows you enable **plugins** for the block. At the time of writing there appears to be only the one plugin available called the **repository** plugin. The repository plugin allows teachers to copy activities and resources to and from a repository on the web. This could be useful in order to share activities and resources between sites. If you don't think this will be useful, you might want to turn this off to avoid confusing teachers. To disable the plugin, hold the *Ctrl* key and click on **repository**, then click on the button labeled **Save Changes**.

Once the block is installed and its global settings have been saved, you can add the block by selecting **Sharing Cart** from the **Blocks** menu. The block only appears to teachers, course creators, and administrators, and is only displayed when editing is turned on.

After adding an instance of the Sharing Cart block to a course page you will also notice a new icon next to each activity and resource in the central column of your course page.

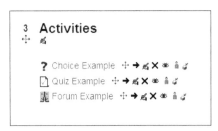

This new icon allows you to add a copy of an item to the Sharing Cart. Items are copied without user data, so assignment submissions, forum posts, and so on, are left with the original and not copied.

When an item is copied to the **Sharing Cart** it appears in a list:

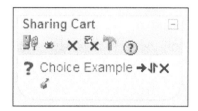

To copy an item from another course, simply go to that course and copy the item. This applies to other teachers' courses as well, so long as you are allowed access to their course.

The **Sharing Cart** can hold a large number of copied items. Items initially appear in the order they were copied, with recent items at the top, however you can reorder items by clicking the up-down icon.

Items can be organized into folders by clicking the right-facing arrow icon; if no folders exist a textbox is presented to allow a new folder to be created; previously created folders can be selected from a drop-down list.

With an item in the **Sharing Cart**, it is possible to clone the item to a course. Clicking the icon that appears as a cube with an outgoing arrow creates a number of target locations in the central column:

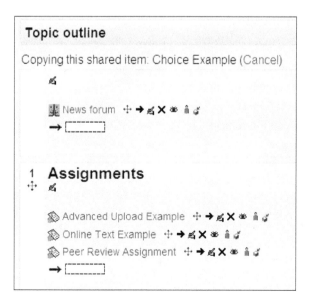

To clone the activity, click on one of the target locations. With the cloned activity copied to a section of the central column, it can be shifted up or down as needed. While the target locations are displayed, you can cancel the copy by clicking on the **Cancel** link at the top of the page.

## How it works...

The **Sharing Cart** utilizes the backup and restore functionality built into most activities and resources. It therefore works for all standard activities and resources, although there are known complications with quiz questions. For a work-around for quizzes, see the online documentation for the block.

The Sharing Cart may also work with contributed modules, although you will want to test this. The commonly used Feedback module (discussed in *Chapter 7, Organizing Students*) has been tested by the Sharing Cart authors, and the Peer Review assignment type worked during this author's testing. Not all contributed modules have backup and restore capabilities.

While modules appear in the **Sharing Cart** block they are kept as `zip` files in the server's file system. This is unlikely to cause space issues as course files associated with activities and resources are stored separately in the file system.

# Searching for users

| Name | Quickfind User List |
|---|---|
| **Module type** | Block |
| **Author** | Mike Worth |
| **Released** | 2009 |
| **Maintained** | Limited |
| **Languages** | English |
| **Compliance** | Good |
| **Documentation** | Online documentation |
| **Errors** | None displayed |

The phone rings—it's a student with a question about the course. You want to quickly look up the student's profile and check their activity. To achieve this you have to go to the participants list, and because there you have a large number of students, they don't all fit on the same screen, so narrow down the search by name or skip from page to page. Eventually you get to a page containing the student's name; you have to scroll and visually search until you find the student's name. Once the name is found, you can click to show the student's profile. So a simple, quick search for a profile can take 30 seconds.

The Quickfind User List block allows you to track down a student, or any user associated with a course, quickly. Just start typing and the block matches users on the fly.

## Getting ready

Unzip and copy the `quickfindlist` block directory into the `/moodle/blocks/` directory, then visit the **Notifications** page.

## How to do it...

Once installed, the block can be added by selecting **Quickfind List** from the **Blocks** menu.

The block can be added to course pages and also on the site's root page or My Moodle pages. When added to a course, the block searches among users in that course. When added to the site root page (the first page linked in the breadcrumb trail), the block searches globally.

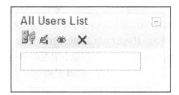

Once added, the block can be used without changing any settings, but if you wish, the settings can be modified on the configuration page for the block.

**Configuring a Quickfind List block**

| | |
|---|---|
| Role for listed people to have | All Users |
| User data to display/search, You can use the following placeholders: | |
| • [[firstname]] • [[lastname]] • [[username]] | [[firstname]] [[lastname]] |
| Page to link to (the person's id will be appended to the end). Leave blank for default profile | |
| Save changes | |

The first setting controls which users will appear in search results. This allows searches to be limited to users of a particular role, for example teachers or students.

It is possible to add more than one instance of the block on the same page. This allows for the possibility to search for teachers or students from separate blocks on the same page. This would probably be more applicable when the block is used on the site's root page. When the role value in this setting changes, the title of the block changes accordingly to match it.

The second setting allows control over how users' names will appear in the search results. By default names are shown with **firstname** followed by **lastname**. This may not be appropriate in all cultures, so the order of these name parts can be rearranged. You can also add a user's username to their name. Where there is a long list of users and possible name duplication, this may provide a means of distinguishing users. To allow searching by user ID, the `[[userid]]` field must be included in this setting.

When a list of users is displayed, each user's name acts as a link to their profile. Leaving the third setting blank achieves this default behavior. If you want the link to direct to something other than a profile, you can put a URL in this setting, leaving space at the end of the URL for an appropriate user ID to be appended. For ideas on how to exploit this setting, see the *There's more...* section of this recipe.

The block functions in the same way for all users, including both teachers and students. If you wish to restrict access to the block so that only teachers can use it, click on the **Assign roles** icon, which is the top-left icon displayed on the block header, while editing is turned on. Click on the **Override Permissions** tab, then you can alter the **View** permission setting for each role as you see fit.

You may have to **Turn editing off** before you can test the block.

## How it works...

The block initially appears blank except for a textbox to enter a search string. As the user types, the list of names containing characters corresponding to the user's search string appear. The list appears dynamically and quickly without reloading the page.

Behind the scenes as the page loads, the block pre-loads a list of all users and hides them. As the user types, a JavaScript function matches users against the string provided and reveals any matching entries.

As names appear, they can be clicked and, by default, the user is taken to the profile page for that user.

## There's more...

The block can be used for a number of applications:

- Searching for teachers globally in a site
- Searching for administrators who can assist you with technical problems
- Allowing teachers to search for students, and students to search for fellow students

### Directing to other user related resources

By default, clicking on a name in the search results directs you to the user profile for that user. It is possible to configure the block to direct to other pages.

In a reflective course or site, blogging may be a central part of the student experience. To direct to the blog of the user, use the following URL in the third block setting field. Replace `localhost/moodle/` with the URL of your site's web root: `http://localhost/moodle/blog/index.php?userid=`.

In a social course, forums may be the focus of activity. To search for posts by user, use the following URL in the third setting field. Replace `localhost/moodle/` with the URL of your site's web root and replace the value of the `id` attribute with the course code for the current course: `http://localhost/moodle/mod/forum/search.php?id=2&search=userid:`.

### Tidying up the user list

The search results list appears with bullet points overhanging the block in some browsers or no bullets at all in other browsers. To bring the bullet points inside the block, the style for each item can be modified where it is changed. Open the file `quickfindlist.js` and find the last statement. It appears as follows:

```
person.style.display="list-item";
```

To bring bullets inside the block, add a statement immediately following the preceding one:

```
person.style.marginLeft="1em";
```

If you don't want bullets at all, you can replace the preceding `list-item` statement with the following statement:

```
person.style.display="block";
```

# Measuring dedication

| | |
|---|---|
| **Name** | Course Dedication block |
| **Module Type** | Block |
| **Author** | Borja Rubio Reyes |
| **Released** | 2008 |
| **Maintained** | Actively |
| **Languages** | English, German, Portuguese Brazilian, Spanish |
| **Compliance** | Good |
| **Documentation** | None |
| **Errors** | None displayed |

If you are attempting to gauge a student's involvement in the course, you can look at their activity, but this doesn't really show how dedicated they have been in visiting your site and participating in your online course.

The Course Dedication block estimates how long a student has spent online by examining logs and looking for contiguous periods of user activity.

## Getting ready

The download link for the module takes you to the author's site, from where you can download the module. Once you have it, unzip and copy the block directory into the `/moodle/blocks/` directory, then visit the **Notifications** page.

## How to do it...

You can add the Course Dedication block by selecting **Course dedication** from the **Blocks** menu. When it is added it is only visible to teachers and administrators.

There are no settings associated with the block. In fact there is only one action you can take with the block, and that is to click the **Calculate...** link. The block is simply a launch-pad to pages that query student dedication.

First, a page appears that allows the teacher to select the period of time over which the dedication query will be conducted.

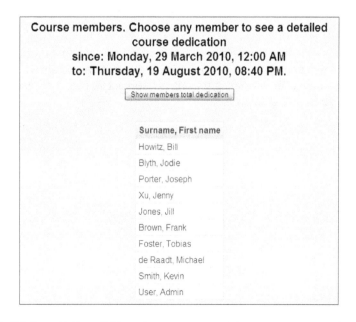

By default, the time period starts at the beginning of the course (the nominal course start date) and ends at the current time. The query can be narrowed by adjusting the start and end of the period to specify another period of time, for instance, the last week or month.

The query estimates that a user has been online if they have log entries relating to activities (clicks) spanning no more than a specified time gap. The default for this gap is 60 minutes; in other words, if a user clicks once, then again 59 minutes later, they are seen as having been online during the intervening time period. The granularity of this as a measure of online use can be adjusted by increasing or reducing this figure; a smaller figure assumes greater activity, a larger figure allows for greater periods of inactivity during online periods.

With a timeframe for the query in place, and the activity gap specified, you can proceed to the next step:

A table of users is shown, including students, teachers, and administrators. At this point, you can choose to show the dedication of a single user by clicking on their name, or you can show the dedication of all users involved in a course by clicking the button labeled **Show members total dedication**. Assuming you choose the latter option, a table of all users and their time online is displayed:

---

**Course members. Choose any member to see a detailed course dedication**
**since: Monday, 29 March 2010, 12:00 AM**
**to: Thursday, 19 August 2010, 08:40 PM.**

Download in Excel format

| Surname, First name | Course dedication |
| --- | --- |
| Howitz, Bill | 0 minutes |
| Blyth, Jodie | 0 minutes |
| Porter, Joseph | 2 minutes |
| Xu, Jenny | 3 minutes |
| Jones, Jill | 12 minutes |
| Brown, Frank | 14 minutes |
| Foster, Tobias | 30 minutes |
| de Raadt, Michael | 1 hours and 18 minutes |
| Smith, Kevin | 2 hours and 28 minutes |
| User, Admin | 10 hours and 43 minutes |

---

From this page, a spreadsheet can be downloaded, which contains the data presented on the page. Also from this page, the individual user's dedication can be shown by clicking on a user's name. For a single user, assuming they have been active over a number of sessions, the length of each session is displayed:

**Course dedication of Tobias Foster**
**since: Monday, 29 March 2010, 12:00 AM**
**to: Thursday, 19 August 2010, 08:40 PM.**

**Total dedication:** 30 minutes

| Session start | Duration |
| --- | --- |
| Saturday, 10 July 2010, 12:05 PM | 18 minutes |
| Saturday, 10 July 2010, 04:27 PM | 1 minutes |
| Saturday, 10 July 2010, 06:17 PM | 9 minutes |

## See also

- Usage block
- User Growth block
- Graph Stats block

# Getting user statistics

| Name | Usage | User Growth Block | Graph Stats |
| --- | --- | --- | --- |
| **Module Type** | Block | Block | Block |
| **Author** | José Coelho | Valery Fremaux, Emeline Daude | Eric Bugnet |
| **Released** | 2008 | 2009 | 2006 |
| **Maintained** | Actively | Limited | Actively |
| **Languages** | Basque, Catalan, English, German, Hebrew, Hungarian, Portuguese | English, French | English, French, Hungarian, Polish, Russian |
| **Compliance** | Good | OK | Good |
| **Documentation** | Online documentation | None | None |
| **Errors** | Errors displayed with error reporting turned on | None displayed | None displayed |

Sometimes there is a need to get a broader picture of what is going on. How many students are there? How many users have used the site recently? How often are users connecting? There are a number of blocks that attempt to answer these questions.

## Getting ready

The Graph Stats block needs to be downloaded from the author's website. The Usage and User Growth blocks are downloaded as normal from `http://moodle.org/`.

Once you have all the blocks, unzip them and copy the block directories into the `/moodle/blocks/` directory, then visit the **Notifications** page.

## How to do it...

The Usage and User Growth blocks each have global settings, but you need not change them in order to use these blocks. The Graph Stats block will force you to view and save the global settings when the block is installed. When shown in Moodle, the Graph Stats block is referred to simply as **Statistics**.

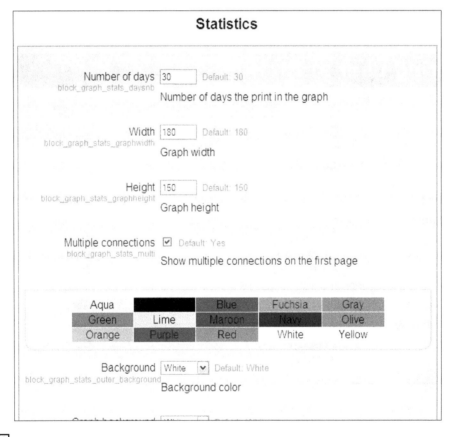

You can accept these settings and save them as it is. If you wish the graph to show a shorter or longer period than **30** days, you can change this default. The setting labeled **Multiple connections** controls the counts of connections. Each day the number of individual users who connected is shown; the block can also show the total number of connections (including reconnections) on the same day. The remaining settings relate to the presentation of the block and its embedded graph.

These three blocks are primarily intended to be shown on the site root page. They can be used on course pages, but they may not perform as you would expect on those pages; connections and user numbers are really site-wide figures.

Each block can be added from the **Blocks** menu. The Usage block is titled **Usage**, the User Growth block is titled **Active users**, and the Graph Stats block is labeled **Statistics**.

When the blocks are added to the site root page, they can be viewed by everyone, even users who are not logged on. If you are running a live site, you may want to limit who can view the blocks by changing view permissions for various users. You can access these permissions by clicking the icon labeled **Assign roles** in the header of each block, going to the **Override Permissions** tab, selecting each user role you wish to change and altering the **View block** capability of each role in turn.

Of the three blocks, only the Usage block has any instance settings. Clicking on the configuration icon for that block will show the following settings:

| Configuring a Usage block | | |
|---|---|---|
| Months: 12 ▾ | Days: 30 ▾ | Hours: 24 ▾ |
| Default: Days ▾ | Width: 200 | Height: 100 |
| Pageviews | Users: | Messages: |
| 1 ▾ Bar ▾ blue ▾ | 1 ▾ Line ▾ orange ▾ | 1 ▾ Line ▾ green ▾ |
| | Save changes | |

The row and column layout of this collection of settings is a little misleading. The top two rows are independent of the rows below.

The block can show usage statistics over three timeframes: months, days, and hours. The length of these timeframes can be adjusted independently by changing the settings in the top row.

The second row of settings controls the appearance of the block including the initial view and the dimensions of the graph inside the block.

The bottom two rows control how the three measured statistics are presented. Each aspect can be turned on and off using the first **1/0** setting. Each count can be presented as a horizontal line, a vertical bar, or as a filled area. The color of each statistic can also be chosen.

## How it works...

When the Usage block has been added, it shows the following:

- The number of page views
- The number of users who connected
- The number of forum posts made

The statistics appear, as defined, with the most recent statistics appearing on the right of the graph and earlier statistics displayed working towards the left:

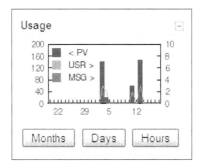

At the bottom of the block there are three buttons. These control the timeframe displayed in the graph. The default view is days, so the last 30 calendar days are shown. Clicking either **Months** or **Hours** shows a different graph for those timeframes, without reloading the page.

The User Growth block shows the number of users in the system over the last 12 calendar months. Each vertical bar indicates the number of users who had accounts created in that month or earlier, in other words, the graph is cumulative over time:

The timeframe can be shifted backwards in time, so you can see how growth happened during earlier years. You can also view periods forward in time and doing so assumes the current number of users will continue (unless the authors have some special code that can look into the future). With a new timeframe set, clicking on the button labeled **Change** will reload the page with the selected timeframe displayed.

The Graph Stats block shows connection statistics over the last month (or set number of days). The graph shows the number of unique users who connected each day, and the total number of connections made (which will differ from the number of users if users log in more than once on a day).

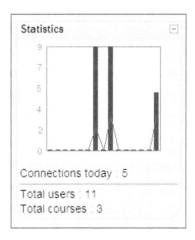

At the bottom of the block the total number of users with current accounts in the system is shown, together with a count of courses on the site; this count includes the root page (which is treated as a limited course within the system).

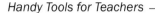

- ▶ Course Dedication block

# 11
# Just for Fun

In this chapter, we will cover:

- ▶ Remembering birthdays
- ▶ Using emoticons
- ▶ Playing with themes
- ▶ Rewarding students
- ▶ Just playing games

## Introduction

Education need not be dull and boring all the time. This chapter is about the extras that make learning that bit more exciting.

### Remembering birthdays

Part of learning is being a member of a learning community. One way to familiarize members with each other is to share the excitement of birthdays. With a little poking and prodding, Moodle can be used to keep track of users' dates of birth, and using these, there is a block that can show you who is celebrating a birthday today or in the near future.

- ▶ Birthday block

## Using emoticons

Emoticons are short pictorial expressions that can enliven a text message. The emoticon icons available in the Skype instant messenger have been made available and can be inserted into Moodle text when the appropriate filter is installed.

- Skype icons filter

## Playing with themes

One of the things that many users love doing is fiddling with colors and themes. Moodle allows the theme of the site to be altered and a number of themes are distributed with Moodle. It is therefore a simple matter to switch themes and there is one block that allows a user to achieve this, without any lasting damage.

- Session Theme Switcher block

## Rewarding students

Learning is a little more fun when there's a small incentive to achieve something physical: "Hey mum! Look what I got!" Here are a couple of modules that will give students something to show off.

- Certificate module
- Stamp Collection module

## Just playing games

Often, there are times when some students have finished their work while others are still plodding along. How do you keep such students from becoming listless while they are idle? Why not allow them the privilege of playing a game (and in the process, they might even learn something without knowing they are learning).

- Game module
- A tutorial on creating a game in a block

# Celebrating birthdays

| | |
|---|---|
| **Name** | Birthday block |
| **Module type** | Block |
| **Author** | Anthony Borrow |
| **Released** | 2007 |
| **Maintained** | Actively |
| **Languages** | Czech, English, English (US), French, French (Canadian), Gallego, German, German (Personal), Italian, Japanese, Portuguese, Slovak, Spanish (numerous variants), Swedish |
| **Compliance** | Good |
| **Documentation** | `Readme.txt` file |
| **Errors** | None displayed |

"Happy Birthday! It's your special day". That's what this block is all about. This block is a great way to celebrate the birthdays of class members and teachers.

Anthony Borrow is Moodle's "CONTRIB Co-ordinator", that means he co-ordinates code contributed to Moodle, among other things. All the module offerings reviewed in this book, that have been published in the last three years or so, have come before his eyes, and have been advised by his experience. The most amazing thing is that Anthony does this significant and necessary work voluntarily, despite offers of payment.

Anthony was asked to take on the role of CONTRIB co-ordinator after he contributed the Birthday block. Anthony was an early Moodle adopter. He has experience as an IT professional and continues to assist in the running of Moodle sites at a number of schools.

Apart from being a true Moodler, Anthony also leads an inspiring life as a Jesuit Priest, living in the United States. He speaks Spanish and is interested in Tai-Chi.

## Getting ready

Unzip and copy the `birthday` block directory into the `/moodle/blocks/` directory, then visit the **Notifications** page.

## How to do it...

Before adding this block to courses, there are a few steps that must be taken at the site level. First, visit the block's global configuration page at **Site Administration | Modules | Blocks | Birthday**.

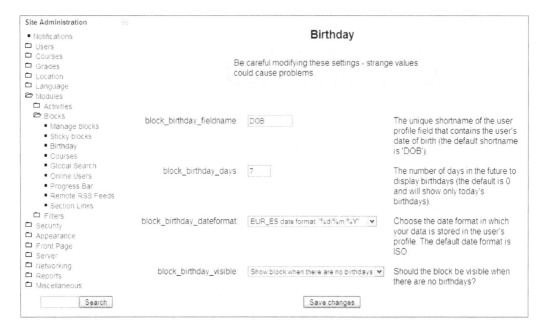

There are four settings on the configuration page:

1. The first you can leave as is, but take note of the value for this setting, as you will need it later. The default is **DOB**.

2. The second setting relates to the future time period for which birthdays are shown, in other words, how far into the future birthdays are checked. The default value is zero, which means birthdays occurring on the current date are shown. You can probe further by setting another value, for example seven days to look a week ahead.

3. The third setting allows you to adjust the format of date values expected on your site. This may vary according to your location and culture, but may also depend on how dates are copied if they are sourced from another system.

   ❑ The final setting allows you to control whether or not the block will appear when there are no birthdays to display. You may wish to save space if there are no birthdays, but this behavior is not the norm. It may confuse teachers if the block does not appear after they add it, just because there are no upcoming birthdays.

Save the changes to the Birthday block's global settings, then navigate to **Site Administration | Users | Accounts | User profile fields**. Here you will add a profile field for users' dates of birth:

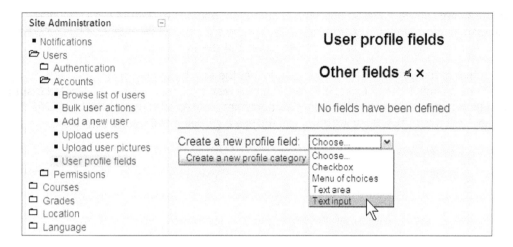

In the drop-down list labeled **Create a new profile field** select the **Text input** option. You should be redirected to a new page in order to specify the new profile field:

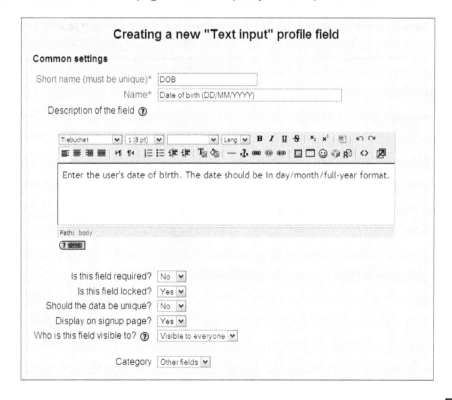

The **Common settings** section has a number of settings you will need to change. The **Short name** should reflect the setting specified earlier in the Birthday block's global settings; the default there was DOB.

For the **Name** setting, enter an appropriate name that equates to **Date of birth**. You may also wish to add some prompt that indicates how the date should be entered if it is entered manually. You may also wish to add a description, but this is not seen by users.

The author of the Birthday block recommends that the field be locked. This means that it cannot be changed after it is first entered. You may wish to change the setting labeled **Display on signup page** depending on how user accounts are created on your site. If self-enrolment is possible, set this to **Yes**. Scrolling down you will see a grouping of **Specific settings**.

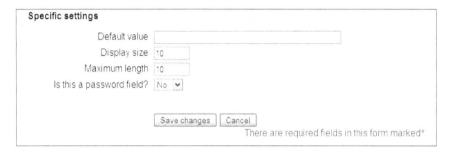

Leave the **Default value** setting blank. Set the **Display size** and **Maximum length** settings to **10** to accommodate sufficient characters for dates, including date-part separators. Save these settings and this field should now appear at the bottom of each user's **Edit profile** page.

**Other fields**

Date of birth (DD/MM/YYYY) [        ]

[ Update profile ]

There are required fields in this form marked*

With this field in place, it is also possible to include the field when creating accounts by uploading users.

You will only need to make these site-wide changes once. Afterwards, teachers can add the Birthday block as they see fit by selecting **Birthday** from the **Blocks** menu.

## How it works...

Once added to a course page (assuming user's birthdays have been entered) the Birthday block will display current and upcoming birthdays. If there are no birthdays to show, the block will either be absent, or show the following (depending on the block's global visibility setting):

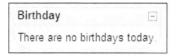

When there are people having birthdays on the current day or (if a number of days has been specified) in coming days, they will be presented with their name and profile picture:

Clicking on a user's name shows their profile. Clicking on the envelope below the user's profile allows someone to send a birthday greeting using the messaging facility.

# Adding emotions

| Name | Skype icons |
|---|---|
| **Module type** | Filter |
| **Author** | Martin Dougiamas |
| **Released** | 2008 |
| **Maintained** | Actively |
| **Languages** | English |
| **Compliance** | Good |
| **Documentation** | `Readme.txt` file |
| **Errors** | None displayed |

Do you want to allow more emotions in your text? A picture is worth a thousand words. An emoticon is probably worth less than that, but it's certainly more fun (smile).

## Getting ready

Unzip and copy the `skypeicons` directory into the `/moodle/filter/` directory.

## How to do it...

Once the files are in place, you will need to enable this filter at **Site Administration | Modules | Filters | Manage filters**:

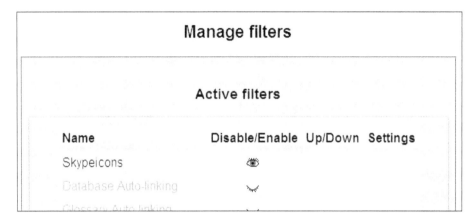

| Manage filters | | | |
| --- | --- | --- | --- |
| **Active filters** | | | |
| Name | Disable/Enable | Up/Down | Settings |
| Skypeicons | 👁 | | |
| Database Auto-linking | | | |
| Glossary Auto-linking | | | |

Click on the eye icon in the row named **Skypeicons** so that it appears as an open eye. It will then be possible to add Skype icons around your site.

Skype icons are added by using appropriate code strings enclosed in parentheses. Emoticons can be added anywhere you can add text content. This includes labels, web pages, forum posts, assignment descriptions, and so on.

Possible emoticon tags are: (angel) (angry) (bandit) (beer) (bigsmile) (blush) (bow) (brokenheart) (cake) (call) (cash) (clapping) (coffee) (cool) (crying) (dance) (devil) (doh) (drink) (drunk) (dull) (envy) (evilgrin) (flower) (giggle) (handshake) (headbang) (heart) (hi) (hug) (inlove) (itwasntme) (kiss) (lipssealed) (mail) (makeup) (middlefinger) (mmm) (mooning) (movie) (muscle) (music) (nerd) (ninja) (no) (party) (phone) (pizza) (puke) (rain) (rock) (sadsmile) (skype) (sleepy) (smile) (smoke) (speechless) (star) (sun) (surprised) (sweating) (talking) (thinking) (time) (toivo) (tongueout) (wait) (wink) (wondering) (worried) (yawn) (yes)

## How it works...

The icons appear rendered as animated emoticons. They are cute and colorful, but beware, some are a little rude (notably, these rude icons are not shown on the **Modules and plugins** entry for the Skype icons filter):

Moving the mouse over each emoticon shows the code used to add it to the text.

## There's more...

One must wonder if there is anything of educational value in emoticons, but perhaps there may be. Emoticons have emerged as another form of txt spk (text speak) that is worth study within the fields of language expression and popular culture.

### Censoring emoticons

If you feel that some of the emoticons may cause offense or may be inappropriate for students at your institution, you can selectively remove particular emoticons by editing the filter file / moodle/filter/skypeicons/filter.php.

At line 22 you will find an array declared with a string value for each emoticon. Remove the strings for the emoticons you wish to banish.

```
$images = array('angel', 'angry', 'bandit', 'beer', ...
```

# Theme swapping

| Name | Session Theme Switcher |
|---|---|
| **Module type** | Block |
| **Author** | Shane Elliott |
| **Released** | 2007 |
| **Maintained** | Limited |
| **Languages** | English |
| **Compliance** | OK |
| **Documentation** | None |
| **Errors** | None displayed |

If you have a strict corporate institutional site, then there has probably been a lot of thought put into making your theme in order to achieve effective "branding". Fiddling with this might be worth your job. However, if you are not bound by such restrictions, then perhaps you are able to offer users some choice in the look and feel of your site.

The Session Theme Switcher block allows users to change the theme used on a site for the duration of their session in Moodle. The capability for switching themes is limited to teachers and administrators, but could even be extended to other users.

## Getting ready

Unzip and copy the block directory into the /moodle/blocks/ directory, but don't visit the **Notifications** page yet. Delete the install.xml and upgrade.php files from the /moodle/blocks/session_theme/db directory, leaving the access.php file. After deleting these files, you can then visit the **Notifications** page.

## How to do it...

With the code in place, there is another setting you need to add. Open the /moodle/config.php file. This is the global configuration file. Add the following line to the file, after the initial unset() function call.

```
$CFG->allowthemechangeonurl = 1;
```

You will then be able to add the **Session Theme** block from the **Blocks** menu. Add the block to the site root page; when added to course pages, it does change the theme, but does not return the user to the course, which could be confusing.

To allow users other than teachers and administrators to change their session theme, you can modify the permissions at **Site Administration | Users | Permissions | Define roles**. Editing the permissions of the "Authenticated user" role will have an effect on all users. The **Switch themes** permission controls the ability to use this block.

## How it works...

When installed, the block allows the user to select a theme by name from a list:

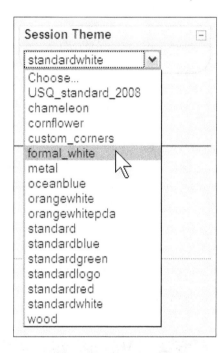

When a new theme is selected, the page reloads with the new theme appearing:

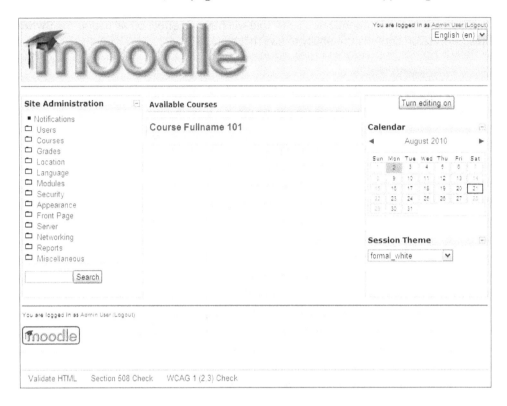

After the user logs out and returns to the site, the theme returns to the site's nominated theme.

# Awarding certificates

| Name | Certificate |
|---|---|
| **Module type** | Activity module |
| **Author** | Chardelle Busch |
| **Released** | 2007 |
| **Maintained** | Actively |
| **Languages** | English, Gallego, German, Italian, Portuguese Brazilian, Romanian, Spanish |
| **Compliance** | Good |
| **Documentation** | Online documentation, help files |
| **Errors** | None displayed |

Certificates for completing a course could be considered as a fun addition, or it could be quite a serious aspect. The certificate module allows students to generate certificates that they can keep electronically or print out. This module is highly configurable and can be linked to course grades or assessment outcomes.

 The Certificate module is one of the most downloaded contributed modules for Moodle. This is not surprising as the module is a great example of a well-designed and useful module. To see statistics about contributed module downloads, visit `http://download.moodle.org/stats.php`.

## Getting ready

Unzip and copy the `certificate` directory into the `/moodle/mod/` directory, then visit the **Notifications** page.

## How to do it...

Once installed, you can add the Certificate module as an Activity by selecting **Certificate** from the **Add an activity...** menu.

Once created, you will be taken to the configuration page for a Certificate activity:

▸ The **Certificate Name** field becomes the link title on the course main page. The introduction appears on the page from which the certificate is downloaded. All students can reach the page that allows them to download a certificate, but only students who meet the set requirements will be able to download their certificate. If a student is ineligible they are told why, but successful students are not informed about why they have been successful. It may be wise to write what is required from students in the **Introduction**.

▸ In the second group of settings(**Issue Options**), there are settings related to how a certificate is issued to a student. The certificates are produced as PDF files, generated by the system. Teachers can be alerted when a certificate is produced by a student if the first setting, labeled **Email Teachers**, is set to **Yes**. Other people, such as a school principal can also be alerted, by typing their e-mail address into the field of the second setting. Multiple e-mail addresses can be added, separated by commas. The setting labeled **Delivery** allows you to control how the student receives the PDF file. You can allow the student to download the certificate when it is generated or the file can be e-mailed to the student. Students can always come back and re-issue a new certificate if needed. The final setting in this grouping controls the saving of certificate PDF files on the server. If certificates are saved, the teacher can view them using the Certificates Report (described later).

Scrolling down there are more options:

**Locking Options**

| | |
|---|---|
| Required course grade ⑦ | 50% ⌄ |
| Minimum required minutes in course ⑦ | 0 |
| Dependent activities ⑦ | Linked Activity      Required Grade |
| 1 | -- none --         ⌄  No  ⌄ |
| | Add another linked activity option |

**Text Options**

| | |
|---|---|
| Print Date ⑦ | Date Received ⌄ |
| Date Format ⑦ | January 1, 2000 ⌄ |
| Print Code ⑦ | No ⌄ |
| Print Grade ⑦ | Topic 1 . Peer Review Assignment Grade ⌄ |
| Grade Format ⑦ | Percentage Grade ⌄ |
| Print Outcome ⑦ | No ⌄ |
| Print Credit Hours ⑦ | |
| Print Teacher Name(s) ⑦ | No ⌄ |
| Custom Text ⑦ | |

- The **Locking Options** specify the requirements a student must meet before they can be issued a certificate for completing the course. The requirements can be based around three factors: course grade, time spent online, and/or satisfactory completion of one or more assessment items (quizzes and assignments). Combinations of these can be created with all specified requirements needing to be met.

- The **Text Options** describe the information added to the certificate. The first setting labeled **Print Date** controls which date is added to the certificate. This setting has options for being no date, the date the certificate is produced, or the date of the end of the course (which must be set in the course settings). If a date is to be added to the certificate, one of the number of formats can be selected in the following setting.

- Each certificate has a code of ten random letters and numbers associated with it. If there is a possibility that certificates could be modified or forged by students, this code can be added to certificates and then later matched to issued certificates as a means of verification. The **Print Code** setting controls whether or not this code is printed on certificates.

- A grade value can optionally be added to the certificate. This can be the course grade or a single grade from one assessment item. The **Print Grade** setting controls this. Unfortunately, you cannot add multiple grade values to a certificate. The format of the grade can be set as being a raw mark, a percentage, or a grade value, as specified by the following setting.

**Letter Grades**

Grade letter values are set at the site level. For information about setting letter grades, visit `http://docs.moodle.org/en/Grade_letters`.

- If outcomes have been specified in your course, these can be added to a certificate by changing the **Print Outcome** setting.

- A number of **Credit Hours** can be printed to the certificate. This might be useful if on completion of one course, a student is rewarded with a gift of credit that can be used towards another course or perhaps some form of free time in class.

  Teacher names can be added to the certificate. The module uses the teachers defined for the course (users who have the teacher role). Additional teachers can be added by assigning them to the teacher role for the module instance. To do this, go to the settings for the Certificate activity and click the tab labeled **Locally assigned roles**. Click on the **Teacher** role and **Add** users from the list on the right to the one on the left.

- The final setting in the **Text Options** grouping allows you to specify additional **Custom Text** that can be printed to the certificate. This text does not override any other text shown on the certificate and does not appear with any great prominence. This might be useful for a small annotation on the certificate.

At the bottom of the Certificate configuration page there are some more settings:

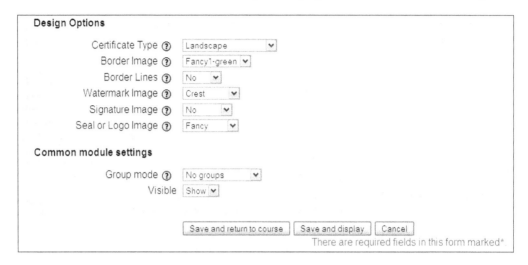

- ▸ The **Design Options** describe the appearance of the certificate page. The certificate can appear in **Landscape** or **Portrait** orientations in A4 or Letter format. If non-English characters are being used, the Unicode format should be selected.

- ▸ Borders can be added around the certificate, including a number of fancy borders and modern outlines. A watermark image can be added to the background, behind text in the certificate. A signature image can be added to the certificate. To add a new signature, create it as an image file (`jpg` or `png`) and copy the file to `/moodle/mod/certificate/pix/signatures/` This signature is then available site-wide, which may not be appropriate in a large institution. A seal or logo image can be added to certificates. To add a new logo image, copy a `jpg` or `png` image to `/moodle/mod/certificate/pix/seals/`. This would be useful for institutional crests or logos.

With a Certificate activity in place, students can begin to produce their own certificates, provided requirements are met. When a teacher views the Certificate module page, there is a link in the top-right corner to a **Certificates report**.

## Certificates

| Awarded To | Date Received | Grade | Code |
|---|---|---|---|
| Frank Brown | Saturday, 21 August 2010, 11:09 PM | 80.00 % | DDS8QiWsyt |
| Jenny Xu | Saturday, 21 August 2010, 11:23 PM | 80.00 % | m1fiLSTxHw |
| Jill Jones | Saturday, 21 August 2010, 11:21 PM | 100.00 % | qUpMfqHylv |
| Kevin Smith | Saturday, 21 August 2010, 11:20 PM | 90.00 % | jREyxTgRtH |
| Tobias Foster | Saturday, 21 August 2010, 11:21 PM | 70.00 % | QnzN3PV0Rk |

Download in ODS format | Download in Excel format | Download in text format

The Certificates report lists who has been awarded with a certificate, when it was awarded, and what grade was added to the certificate. The code for each certificate is provided and can be matched to a certificate for verification.

## How it works...

From a student's perspective, when they click on the link to the Certificate page they will see whether or not they are eligible to receive a certificate:

**Course Fullname 101**

Michael's ▶ CF101 ▶ Certificates ▶ **Certificate For Completing the Course**

You will receive this certificate if you have successfully passed the course with 50% or more.

Click the button below to save your certificate to your computer.

Get your certificate

If students are eligible they will see the button above and be able to produce their certificate. If they are ineligible, the student is told that their grade is below the required level and no option to produce a certificate is provided.

The certificate is produced as a PDF file, whether it is to be delivered as a web download or using e-mail. The certificate is a somewhat official looking document that the student can keep as a record of their completion of the course.

## See also

▸ Stamp Collection activity module

# Rewarding with gold stars

| | |
|---|---|
| **Name** | Stamp Collection |
| **Module type** | Activity module |
| **Author** | David Mudrák |
| **Released** | 2008 |
| **Maintained** | Actively |
| **Languages** | Catalan, Czech, English, German, Spanish |
| **Compliance** | Good |
| **Documentation** | Online documentation, some help files |
| **Errors** | None displayed |

In many classrooms, cumulative rewards (such as collecting gold stars) are used to motivate students and encourage good behavior. The Stamp Collection module allows teachers to take this type of reward system online.

## Getting ready

Unzip and copy the `stampcoll` directory into the `/moodle/mod/` directory, then visit the **Notifications** page.

## How to do it...

There are not many settings associated with a stamp collection, it's quite simple to set up:

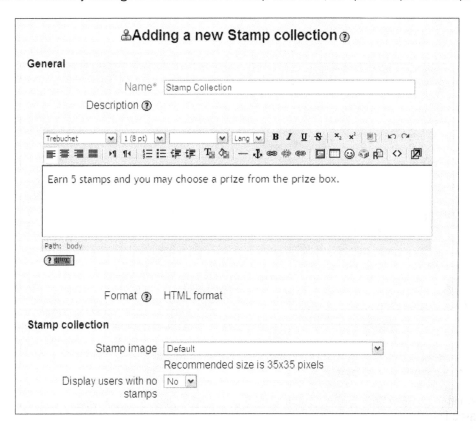

The activity **Name** setting becomes the link to the Stamp Collection on the course page. A description can also be set which will appear at the top of a Stamp Collection page; this is an excellent place to describe the details of your incentive program.

The setting labeled **Stamp image** allows the teacher to select the default image (a gold star, of course) or any image found in the course files area.

The default view for a teacher is the list of users who have been awarded stamps. This can include students who have not yet been awarded stamps if the final setting, labeled **Display users with no stamps** is set to **Yes**.

With the activity in place, a teacher can then begin awarding stamps. Click on the activity link and then click on the **Edit stamps** tab.

Stamps can be awarded by typing a reason for awarding the stamp next to a student's name, then clicking on the **Add** button.

When stamps have been awarded, the **View stamps** tab shows who has been awarded stamps.

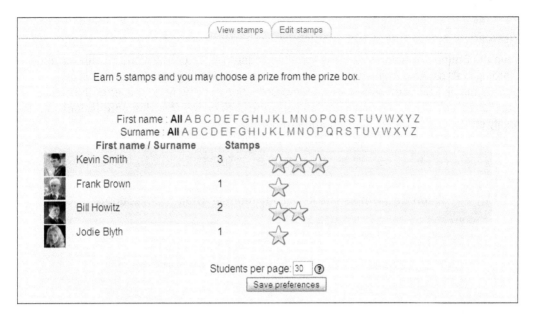

In this view, stamps appear as a star (or another image if selected), without any text. To see details of who awarded the stamp, when, and why, move the mouse over a stamp image.

## How it works...

The student view shows the student the stamps they have been awarded.

The student can also mouse-over their stamps to see why it was awarded and other details.

## There's more...

When the Stamp Collection module is installed, it establishes permissions for viewing and awarding stamps. An administrator or a teacher who has been given this potential can override the default permissions for a Stamp Collection activity. To do this after the activity is established, go back to the configuration page and click on the **Override permissions** tab. To modify student capabilities, click on **Student**.

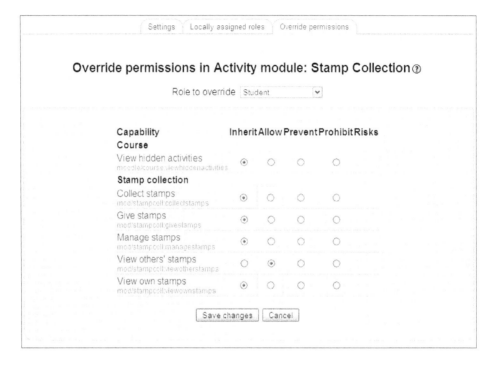

Here are some ideas of how the Stamp Collection module could be used in a teaching situation after modifying permissions:

- Encourage competition by allowing students to see others' stamps. Do this by setting the students' **View others' stamps** permission to **Allow**.
- Encourage collegial behavior by allowing students to award stamps to each other. Do this by setting the students' **Give stamps** permission to **Allow**.

## See also

- Certificate activity module

# Playing games

| | |
|---|---|
| **Name** | Game |
| **Module type** | Activity module |
| **Author** | Vasilis Daloukas |
| **Released** | 2008 |
| **Maintained** | Actively |
| **Languages** | English |
| **Compliance** | Good |
| **Documentation** | Online documentation |
| **Errors** | Some errors displayed with error reporting turned on |

The Game module is mostly about fun, but manages to add learning in as well. It is an excellent teaching resource for students of all ages.

 The Game module does not use Flash, but does use JavaScript for a number of game functions.

## Getting ready

Unzip and copy the `game` directory into the `/moodle/mod/` directory, then visit the **Notifications** page.

## How to do it...

Once installed, the Game module appears as a number of **Games** in the **Add an activity...** list. Choosing one of the game names allows you to set up that form of game in your course.

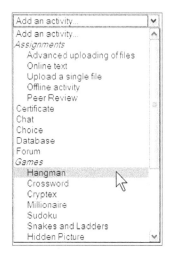

Each game has a number of common settings. The following is the configuration page for a **Hangman** game:

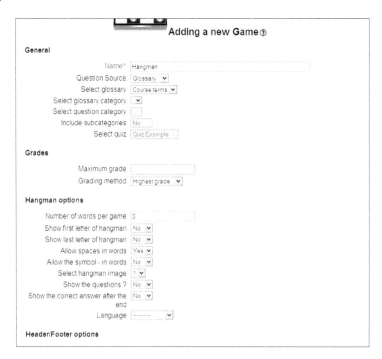

- The **Name** setting value becomes the link text for the game in your course page.

- The remaining **General** settings describe where the source of information for the game will come from. You can choose from pre-existing data stored in either a **Glossary** or **Quiz** questions. Almost all games in the Game module can make use of Glossary entries, matching glossary terms to their definition, or vice versa. Short Answer Quiz questions can be used for the same purpose. Multiple choice and true/false quiz questions can be used in some games.

- Game completion can be used as a grade item in your course. Adding a numeric **Maximum grade** value, other than zero, will cause the game to be included in the course grade items. The **Grading method** setting controls whether the grade is based on the first, last or best attempt, or an average of all attempts.

- The group of settings marked as **Hangman options** are specific to the Hangman game, and how these are adjusted will depend on the maturity of your students. Each type of game in the Games module has its own specific settings, such as these.

- At the end of the configuration page there are settings for adding header and footer text above and below the game.

Once the game is configured, students can begin playing:

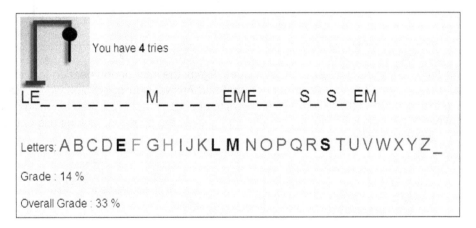

The Crossword game uses entries from a **Glossary** or from Short Answer Quiz questions. Using these it can match terms with definitions to draw up the crossword puzzle:

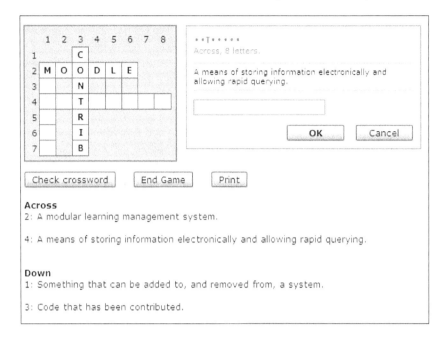

A Cryptex game is a word finding puzzle with clues. Again, the information needed to create the puzzle can be drawn from a **Glossary** or from Short Answer Quiz questions. Words are hidden in the puzzle, and these serve as answers to questions that are asked alongside the puzzle. When a question is asked, the student can answer the question, making use of the words in the puzzle as clues:

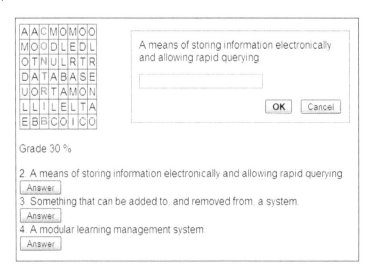

The Millionaire game is based on the television quiz show "Who Wants to be a Millionaire". The game is essentially a multiple choice quiz with a challenge to complete all 15 questions without making an error. As with the television show, there are hints that the student can use, but only once per round. To create a Millionaire game there must be at least 15 multiple choice questions available in a single category of the question bank.

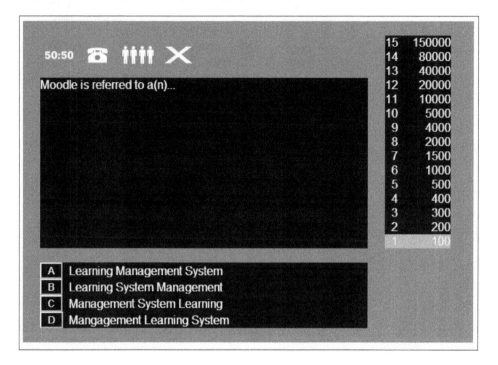

The Sudoku game involves a regular Sudoku game that the student can solve by entering numbers in correct locations. Students can also earn additional number clues by answering questions related to the course. These questions are sourced from a **Glossary**, or from various types of **Quiz** questions:

| 6 | A2 | 8 | 9 | ☐ | 3 | ☐ | ☐ | ☐ |
|---|----|---|---|---|---|---|---|---|
| A4 | 7 | A6 | ☐ | 2 | 4 | ☐ | ☐ | ☐ |
| A7 | A8 | A9 | ☐ | ☐ | ☐ | 9 | 6 | 5 |
| ☐ | 3 | ☐ | ☐ | 7 | ☐ | 8 | 9 | ☐ |
| ☐ | ☐ | ☐ | ☐ | 3 | 6 | ☐ | 7 | ☐ |
| 2 | 8 | ☐ | ☐ | ☐ | ☐ | ☐ | ☐ | ☐ |
| 3 | 9 | 1 | ☐ | ☐ | ☐ | ☐ | ☐ | ☐ |
| ☐ | ☐ | ☐ | ☐ | ☐ | ☐ | 2 | ☐ | 1 |
| ☐ | ☐ | ☐ | 5 | 6 | ☐ | ☐ | ☐ | ☐ |

Grade answers

A2. A system that organises course related resources and activities.

Answer:

A4. Code that has been contributed.
Answer:

A6. A modular learning management system

The Hidden Picture game allows the student to reveal a picture clue, piece by piece, by answering questions correctly. The picture clue should then aid the student to answer the main question for the game. Questions are drawn from a **Glossary** or from **Quiz** questions. One of the questions must have an image attached so that it can become the main question and so that the attached picture can become the picture clue.

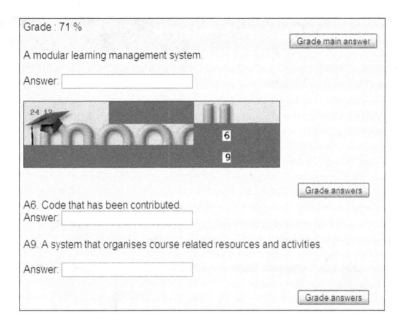

The Snakes and Ladders game resembles the traditional board game of the same name. Players advance by answering course related questions drawn from a **Glossary** or from Short Answer Quiz questions. Each time they answer, the player moves ahead by a random amount and may climb ladders or slide down snakes until they eventually reach the final square.

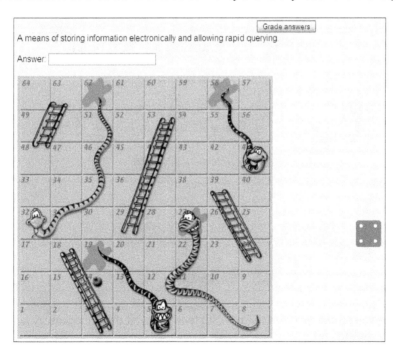

# Creating a game in a block

This section is not a review of a contributed Moodle module; instead it is a quick guide to adding a game in a block in Moodle.

## Getting ready

Find a free Flash game on the web and save it to your computer.

## How to do it...

Copy the Flash game file to the **Files** area of your course in Moodle. Get the web path to the file by right-clicking on the file's name and copying the location of the file.

Go back to the course main page and add an **HTML block** from the **Blocks** menu.

Click on the configuration icon for the block. The configuration page for the block will appear as follows:

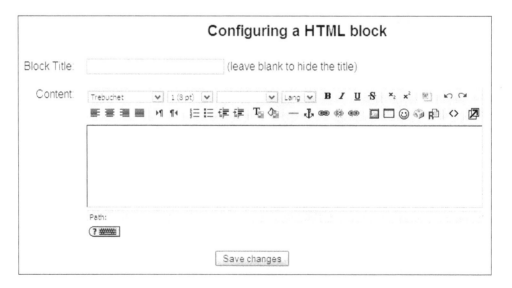

You can add a title for the block, but leaving it blank will omit the unnecessary block header (when editing is turned off).

In the WYSIWYG editor, switch to HTML source mode, by clicking the button on the bottom row of icons, second from the right, with a **< >** symbol on it.

Add the following HTML, replacing the URL `http://localhost/moodle/file.php/2/` `invaders.swf` with the URL of your Flash game file:

```
<object width="190">
<param name="movie" value="http://localhost/moodle/file.php/2/
invaders.swf">
<embed src="http://localhost/moodle/file.php/2/invaders.swf"
width="190">
</embed>
</object>
```

Save changes and when you return to your course page, there should be the Flash game in a block.

 If the Flash game does not look large enough within a 190 pixel width column, you can achieve a similar result in a web page by selecting **Compose a web page** from the **Add a resource...** menu and using the same HTML code.

# Index

## Thank you for buying
# Moodle 1.9 Top Extensions Cookbook

## About Packt Publishing

Packt, pronounced 'packed', published its first book "*Mastering phpMyAdmin for Effective MySQL Management*" in April 2004 and subsequently continued to specialize in publishing highly focused books on specific technologies and solutions.

Our books and publications share the experiences of your fellow IT professionals in adapting and customizing today's systems, applications, and frameworks. Our solution based books give you the knowledge and power to customize the software and technologies you're using to get the job done. Packt books are more specific and less general than the IT books you have seen in the past. Our unique business model allows us to bring you more focused information, giving you more of what you need to know, and less of what you don't.

Packt is a modern, yet unique publishing company, which focuses on producing quality, cutting-edge books for communities of developers, administrators, and newbies alike. For more information, please visit our website: www.packtpub.com.

## About Packt Open Source

In 2010, Packt launched two new brands, Packt Open Source and Packt Enterprise, in order to continue its focus on specialization. This book is part of the Packt Open Source brand, home to books published on software built around Open Source licences, and offering information to anybody from advanced developers to budding web designers. The Open Source brand also runs Packt's Open Source Royalty Scheme, by which Packt gives a royalty to each Open Source project about whose software a book is sold.

## Writing for Packt

We welcome all inquiries from people who are interested in authoring. Book proposals should be sent to author@packtpub.com. If your book idea is still at an early stage and you would like to discuss it first before writing a formal book proposal, contact us; one of our commissioning editors will get in touch with you.

We're not just looking for published authors; if you have strong technical skills but no writing experience, our experienced editors can help you develop a writing career, or simply get some additional reward for your expertise.

## Moodle 1.9 Extension Development

ISBN: 978-1-847194-24-4          Paperback: 320 pages

Customize and extend Moodle using its robust plug-in systems

1. Develop your own blocks, activities, filters, and organize your content with secure code

2. Thoroughly covers key libraries of Moodle and best practices to use them

3. Explore the Moodle architectural concepts, how it is structured, and how it works

4. Detailed examples and screenshots for easy learning

## Moodle 1.9 E-Learning Course Development

ISBN: 978-1-847193-53-7          Paperback: 384 pages

A complete guide to successful learning using Moodle

1. Updated for Moodle version 1.9

2. Straightforward coverage of installing and using the Moodle system

3. Working with Moodle features in all learning environments

4. A unique course-based approach focuses your attention on designing well-structured, interactive, and successful courses

Please check **www.PacktPub.com** for information on our titles

## Moodle 1.9 Multimedia

ISBN: 978-1-847195-90-6          Paperback: 272 pages

Create and share multimedia learning materials in your Moodle courses.

1. Ideas and best practices for teachers and trainers on using multimedia effectively in Moodle

2. Ample screenshots and clear explanations to facilitate learning

3. Covers working with TeacherTube, embedding interactive Flash games, podcasting, and more

4. Create instructional materials and design students' activities around multimedia

## Moodle 1.9 for Design and Technology

ISBN: 978-1-849511-00-1          Paperback: 288 pages

Support and Enhance Food Technology, Product Design, Resistant Materials, Construction, and the Built Environment using Moodle VLE

1. Customize your courses

2. Create a course for each of the key areas of Design and Technology and add material to them

3. Support and assess the progress of the students who are enrolled in the course

4. Use Moodle's detailed and sophisticated gradebook to assess your students' learning progress in activities from assignments to offline activities

Please check **www.PacktPub.com** for information on our titles